Anonymous

Tariff of the Confederate States of America;

Or, Rates of duties, payable on goods, wares and merchandise imported

into the Confederate States, on and after August 31, 1861. Also, United

States tariff of 1861, in parallel columns, alphbetically arran

Anonymous

Tariff of the Confederate States of America;
Or, Rates of duties, payable on goods, wares and merchandise imported into the
Confederate States, on and after August 31, 1861. Also, United States tariff of 1861,
in parallel columns, alphbetically arran

ISBN/EAN: 9783337713669

Printed in Europe, USA, Canada, Australia, Japan

Cover: Foto ©ninafisch / pixelio.de

More available books at **www.hansebooks.com**

TARIFF

OF THE

Confederate States of America;

OR, RATES OF DUTIES,

PAYABLE ON GOODS, WARES AND MERCHANDISE IMPORTED INTO THE CONFEDERATE STATES,

ON AND AFTER AUGUST 31, 1861.

ALSO, UNITED STATES TARIFF OF 1861,

IN PARALLEL COLUMNS.

Alphabetically Arranged.

ALSO,

VALUABLE TABLES OF FOREIGN CURRENCY, WEIGHTS, MEASURES, ETC.

———————

PUBLISHED BY D. H. VAN BUREN & CO.

———————

AUGUSTA, GA:
STEAM PRESS OF CHRONICLE & SENTINEL,
1861.

ADVERTISEMENT.

THE Tariff of the Confederate States herewith presented has been carefully compiled from an official copy of the Act, and the alphabetical arrangement will be found complete. The unusually intricate nature of some of the provisions of the United States' Tariff, renders the work apparently more complicated than necessary for simply mercantile purposes. For various reasons, however, it was deemed advisable to present the two Tariffs in parallel columns, and the wording of the most extended was necessarily adopted.

The Tables of Foreign Currency, Weights, Measures, &c. will be found almost indispensably necessary in our intercourse with European nations.

EXTRACT FROM THE TARIFF OF THE CONFEDERATE STATES.

The nature of some of the provisions of the "free list" of the Tariff of the Confederate States is such, that we deem it best to give the entire list as worded in the Official Act. The articles are also embodied, as far as possible, in the alphabetical arrangement. We give also the following sections of the Act, embracing details and instructions of importance:

[OFFICIAL COPY.]

EXEMPT FROM DUTY.

Books, maps, charts, mathematical and nautical instruments, philosophical apparatus, and all other articles whatever, imported for the use of the Confederate States; books, pamphlets, periodicals, and tracts, published by religious associations.

All philosophical apparatus, instruments, books, maps and charts, statues, statuary, busts and casts of marble, bronze, alabaster, or plaster of Paris, paintings and drawings, etchings, specimens of sculpture, cabinets of coins, medals, gems, and all collections of antiquities; provided the same be specially imported in good faith for the use of any society, incorporated or established for philosophical and literary purposes, or for the encouragement of the fine arts, or for the use or by the order of any church, college, academy, school, or seminary of learning in the Confederate States.

Bullion, gold and silver.

Coins, gold, silver and copper; coffee; cotton; copper, when imported for the mint of the Confederate States.

Garden seeds, and all other seeds for agricultural and horticultural purposes; goods, wares and merchandize, the growth, produce or manufacture of the Confederate States, exported to a foreign country, and brought back to the Confederate States in the same condition as when exported, upon which no drawback has been allowed: *Provided,* That all regulations to ascertain the identity thereof, prescribed by existing laws, or which may be prescribed by the Secretary of the Treasury, shall be complied with; guano, manures and fertilizers of all sorts.

Household effects, old and in use, of persons or families from foreign countries, if used abroad by them, and not intended for any other purpose or purposes, or for sale.

Models or inventions, or other improvements in the arts, provided that no article or articles shall be deemed a model which can be fitted for use.

Paving stones, personal and household effects, not merchandize, of citizens of the Confederate States dying abroad.

Specimens of natural history, minerology, or botany; provided the same be imported in good faith for the use of any society incorporated or established for philosophical, agricultural or horticultural purposes, or for the use or by the order of any college, academy, school, or seminary of learning in the Confederate States.

Wearing apparel, and other personal effects not merchandize; professional books, implements, instruments, and tools of trades, occupation or employment, of persons arriving in the Confederate States; provided that this exemption shall not be construed to include machinery or other articles imported for use in any manufacturing establishment, or for sale.

Bacon, pork, hams, lard, beef, wheat, flour, and bran of wheat, flour and bran of all other grains, Indian corn and meal, barley, rye, oats, and oat meal, and living animals of all kinds, not otherwise provided for; also all agricultural productions, including those of the orchard and garden, in their natural state, not otherwise provided for.

Gunpowder, and all the materials of which it is made.

Lead, in pigs or in bars, in shot or balls, for cannon, muskets, rifles or pistols.

Rags, of whatever material composed.

Arms, of every description, for military purposes, and parts thereof, munitions of war, military accoutrements, and percussion caps.

Ships, steamers, barges, dredging vessels, machinery, screw pile jetties, and articles to be used in the construction of harbors, and for dredging and improving the same.

[EXTRACT.]

SEC. II. *And be it further enacted*, That there shall be levied, collected, and paid, on each and every non-enumerated article which bears a similitude, either in material, quality, texture, or the uses to which it may be applied, to any enumerated article chargeable with duty, the same rate of duty which is levied and charged on the enumerated article by the foregoing schedules, which it most resembles in any of the particulars before mentioned: and if any non-enumerated article equally resembles two or more enumerated articles on which different rates of duty are chargeable, there shall be levied, collected and paid, on such non-enumerated article, the same rate of duty as is chargeable on the article which it resembles, paying the highest duty. *Provided*, That on all articles manufactured from two or more materials, the duty shall be assessed at the highest rates at which any of its component parts may be chargeable. *Provided further*, That on all articles which are not enumerated in the foregoing schedules and cannot be classified under this section, a duty of ten per cent. ad valorem shall be charged.

SEC. III. *And be it further enacted*, That all goods, wares and merchandize, which may be in the public stores as unclaimed, or in warehouse under warehousing bonds, on the 31st day of August next, shall be subject, on entry thereof for consumption, to such duty as if the same had been imported, respectively after that day.

SEC. IV. *And be it further enacted*, That on the entry of any goods, wares or merchandise, imported on or after the 31st day of August aforesaid, the decision of the collector of the customs at the port of importation and entry, as to their liability to duty or exemption therefrom, shall be final and conclusive against the owner, importer, consignee, or agent of any such goods, wares and merchandise, unless, the owner, importer, consignee or agent shall, within ten days after such entry, give notice to the collector, in writing of his dissatisfaction with such decision, setting forth therein distinctly and specifically his ground of objection thereto, and shall, within thirty days after date of such decision, appeal therefrom to the Secretary of the Treasury, whose decision on such appeal shall be final and conclusive: and the said goods, wares and merchandise shall be liable to duty or exemption therefrom accordingly, any act of Congress to the contrary notwithstanding, unless suit shall be brought within thirty days after such decision, for any duties that may have been paid, or may thereafter be paid, on said goods, or within thirty days after the duties shall have been paid in cases where such goods shall be in bond.

SEC. V. *And be it further enacted*, That it shall be lawful for the owner, consignee, or agent of imports which have been actually purchased or procured otherwise than by purchase, on entry of the same, to make such addition in the entry to the cost or value given in the invoice as, in his opinion, may raise the same to the true market value of such imports in the principal markets of the country whence the importations shall have been made, and to add thereto all costs and charges which, under existing laws, would form part of the true value at the port where the same may be entered, upon which the duty should be assessed. And it shall be the duty of the collector within whose district the same may be imported or entered, to cause the dutiable value of such imports to be appraised, estimated and ascertained, in accordance with the provisions of existing laws; and if the appraised value thereof shall exceed by ten per centum, or more, the value so declared on entry, then in addition to the duties imposed by law on the same, there shall be levied, collected and paid a duty of twenty per centum ad valorem, on such appraised value: *Provided nevertheless*, That under no circumstances shall the duty be assessed upon an amount less than the invoice or entered value, and any law of Congress to the contrary notwithstanding.

SEC. VI. *And be it further enacted*, That so much of all acts or parts of acts as may be inconsistent with the provisions of this act shall be and the same are repealed

TARIFFS OF THE CONFEDERATE STATES

(IN EFFECT ON AND AFTER AUGUST 31ST, 1861.)

AND OF THE UNITED STATES,

(IN EFFECT ON AND AFTER APRIL 1st, 1861.)

Alphabetically Arranged.

NOTE.—The Tariff of the Confederate States being altogether *ad valorem*, the figures in the column denote *the rate per cent.*

	C.S.A. Tariff, 1861.	U.S.A. Tariff, 1861.		C.S.A. Tariff 1861.	U.S.A. Tariff, 1861
Absynth...........	25	50c. per gal.	Agates.............	5	5 per cent
Absynth, oil of......	25	30 per cent.	Alabata or German		
Accordions.........	15	20 per cent.	Silver, manufactur		
Acetate of lead.....	15	3c. per lb.	ed or unmanufac-		
Acid, acetic........	10	free	tured....	20	30 per cent
do benzoic........	10	free	Alabaster and spar		
do boracic.......	10	free	ornaments........	25	30 per cent
do chromic......	10	15 per cent	Alba Canella.......	15	20 per cent
do citric.........	10	20 per cent	Alcohol...........	25	
do tartaric.......	10	20 per cent	Alcornoque........	10	free
do muriatic......	10	free	Ale, in bottles......	15	25c. per gal
do nitric, yellow			Ale otherwise than in		
and white....	10	10 per cent	in bottles.........	15	15c. per gal
do oxalic.........	10	10 per cent	Alkanet root.......	5	20 per cent
do pyroligneous..	10	free	Alkermes..........	25	20 per cent
do sulphuric.....	10	free	Allspice..........	20	2c. per lb
do all others for			Allspice, oil of......	15	30 per cent
medicinal pur-			Almonds..........	20	2c. per lb
poses, or in the			do shelled....	20	4c. per lb
fine arts, not			do paste..	25	30 per cent
otherwise pro-			Aloes.............	10	10 per cent
vided for.....	10	10 per cent	Alum, alum substitute		
do all kinds of, used			& Aluminous cake.	15	50c per 100 lbs
for chemical,			Amber............	10	10 per cent
and manufac-			do beads.......	20	30 per cent
turing purp'ses			do oil of.....	15	30 per cent
not other wise			Ambergris.........	10	free
provided for..	10	free	Amethyst..........	5	5 per cent
Adhesive Felt for			Ammonia.........	10	10 per cent
sheathing vessels..	5	free	do sal........	10	10 per cent
Adhesive Plaster salve	15	30 per cent	do carb.......	10	10 per cent
Adzes.............	15	30 per cent	do muriate of..	10	10 per cent

Item	C.S.A. Tariff, 1861	U.S.A. Tariff, 1861	Item	C.S.A. Tariff, 1861	U.S.A. Tariff, 1861
Ammoniac, crude	10	10 per cent	All books, maps, charts and other articles for the use of the Confederate States or of the United States...........	free	free
do refined and hole....	10	20 per cent			
Ammunition, shot(see shot)..............		1½c per lb			
Am'unition, gunpow'r	free	20 per cent	Apparel, wearing, of Wool............	15	12c per lb and 25 per cent
do musket balls.	free	1½c per lb			
Anchors, or parts thereof.......... ...	15	$1.50 per 100 lbs	Apparel, wearing, and other personal baggage in actual use..	free	free
Anchovies in oil.....	25	30 per cent			
do in salt...		(see fish)	Aqua ammonia, hartshorn..........	10	30 per cent
Angelica root.......	15		Aqua Fortis........	10	10 per cent
Angora............	10	20 per cent	Arabic, gum........	10	free
Angora gloves and mits.............	10		Arrack.............	25	50c per gal
Animals, living, of all kinds............	15	30 per cent	Archelia, Archil. or Orchelia....	5	free
Animal oil, of foreign fisheries....	free	free	Argentine...........	20	30 per cent
Animal carbon.......	15	20 per cent	Argol or crude tartar.	10	free
Annatto, Roucou, or Orleans..	10	free	Arms and parts thereof of every description for military purposes........	free	30 per cent
do extract	10	free	Arrow root..........	15	10 per cent
Angora, Thibet, and other Goats or Mohair, unmanufactured............	10	free	Arsenic.............	10	free
Aniseed..........	10	5 per cent	Articles embroidered with gold, silver or other metal......	20	30 per cent
Antimony, crude or regulus of........	10	10 per cent	Apparel, articles worn by men, women or children, of whatever material composed............	15	
Antimony, tartrate of	10	free			
Antique oil........	15	20 per cent			
Antiquities.........	20	30 per cent			
Anvils.............	10	free	Artificial Feathers...	20	30 per cent
	15	$1.25 per 100 lbs	Artificial Flowers....	20	30 per cent
Apparatus, philosophical, books, maps, charts, stationery, &c., spec'ly imported by order, and for the use of any Society, incorporated or established for philosphical or literary purposes, or for the encouragements of the fine arts, or by order and for the use of any college, academy, school, church or seminary of learning	free	free	Ashes, pot, pearl and soda........	10	10 per cent
			Asphaltum....	10	free
			Assafœtida.........	10	10 per cent
			Asses' skin (or parchment)........	15	30 per cent
			Asses' skin, imitation of, or parchment..	15	30 per cent
			Angers.............	15	30 per cent
			Auripigmentum, or orpiment.........	10	free
			Awl Hafts.....	15	30 per cent
			Awls,.............	15	30 per cent
			Axes.............	15	30 per cent
			Axletrees, p'ts therof	15	2c per lb
			Bacon.............	free	2c per lb
			Baggage, personal, in actual use........	free	free

	C.S.A. Tariff, 1861.	U.S.A. Tariff, 1861.
Bagging, cotton, valued at less than 10 cents per square yd.	15	1¼c per lb
Bagging, cotton, valued at over 10 cts per square yard...	15	2c per lb
Bagging, Gunny	15	
Bags, bead, made in part by hand......	15	30 per cent
Bags, grass........	15	30 per cent
do gunny........	15	30 per cent
do woolen......	15	30 per cent
do flax..........	15	
do hemp..........	15	
do carpet, woolen.	15	30 per cent
do silk..........	15	30 per cent
do wool or worst'd and leather ..	15	30 per cent
Baizes.............	15	
Balls, billiard.......	15	30 per cent
do wash.........	25	30 per cent
Balm of Gilead......	15	30 per cent
Balsam Copaiva	20	30 per cent
do Tolu......	20	30 per cent
do medicinal...	20	30 per cent
do all kinds of cosmetic...	20	30 per cent
Bamboos............	10	10 per cent
Bananas............	10	free
Bark of cork trees, unmanufact'ed	10	free
do Peruvian, or bark quilla...	10	10 per cent
do all not otherwise provided for..	10	10 per cent
Barley............	free	15c per bush
do pearl, or hull'd	free	10 per cent
Barege, delaines.....	15	
Barytes, sulphate of..	15	20 per cent
Barwood............	15	free
Bastard Files.......	15	30 per cent
Barilla............	10	free
Baskets, willow.....	15	30 per cent
do wood or ozier	15	30 per cent
do palm leaf.....	15	30 per cent
do straw.......	15	30 per cent
do grass or whale-bone......	15	30 per cent
Battledores.........	15	30 per cent
Bay water or bay rum	20	25c per gal
Bayonets............	free	30 per cent
Bedellium, if crude..	20	free
Beads, all..........	20	30 per cent
Beans, castor.......	15	10 per cent
do tonqua......	15	10 per cent
do vanilla......	15	10 per cent

	C.S.A. Tariff, 1861.	U.S.A. Tariff, 1861.
Beam knives........	15	30 per cent
do scales........	15	30 per cent
Bed-spreads or covers, of the scraps of printed calicoes, sewed..........	15	30 per cent
Bed feathers and feather beds..	15	20 per cent
do ticking, linen...	15	
do ticking, cottton.	15	
do caps..........	15	30 per cent
do screws........	15	1¼c per lb
Beef................	free	1c per lb
Beer, in bottles.....	15	25c per gal
do not in bottles...	15	15c per gal
Beeswax..........	15	10 per cent
Bellows............	15	30 per cent
Bellows pipes.......	15	30 per cent
Belts, sword leather.	free	30 per cent
Benzoin gum.......	15	
Benzoates...........	20	30 per cent
Bell cranks........	15	30 per cent
do levers........	15	30 per cent
do pulls..........	15	30 per cent
do silver.........	20	30 per cent
do gold..........	20	30 per cent
Bells, old, and bell metal............	5	free
Bell metal manufact'd	15	30 per cent
Belts, endless.......	15	25 per cent
Berries used for dyeing, in a crude state.	10	free
Berries, not otherwise provided for......	15	
Bichromate of potash	15	3c per lb
Bick iron...........	15	30 per cent
Billiard and Bagatelle tables, and all other tables and boards on which games are played.........	25	
Binding, woolen....	15	30 per cent
do leather....	15	30 per cent
Birds, singing or other...........	free	free
Bismuth............	10	free
Bitts, carpenters'....	15	30 per cent
Bitter apples.......	10	free
Bitumen............	10	20 per cent
Black, lamp........	15	20 per cent
do lead or plumbago...	15	10 per cent
Blacking............	15	20 per cent
Bladders...........	15	20 per cent
Blacksmiths' hammers	15	2c per lb
do sledges.	15	2c per lb

10

	C.S.A. Tariff, 1861	U.S.A. Tariff, 1861		C.S.A. Tariff, 1861	U.S.A. Tariff, 1861
Blankets of all kinds	15	30 per cent	Bootees, for women or men, silk	15	30 per cent
do wholly or in part of wool not over 28 cts per lb	15	6c per lb and 10 pr ct ad val	Boots, (except India rubber)	15	30 per cent
do above 28 cts per lb and not over 40 cents	15	6c per lb and 25 per cent	Boots laced, silk or satin for children	15	30 per cent
do above 40 cts per lb	15	12c per lb and 20 per cent	Boots and bootees, of leather	15	30 per cent
do for printing and other machines	15	25 per cent	do of all kinds	15	
Bleaching power	10	15c pr 100 lbs	Bookbinders' agates, ferruled	15	20 per cent
Blooms, iron	10	30 per cent	Books, maps, charts, mathematical and nautical instrum'ts, philosophical apparatus and all other articles whatever imported for the use of the Confederate States		free
Boards, planed	10	20 per cent			
do rough	10	20 per cent			
Bobbins	15	30 per cent	Books, pamphlets, periodicals and tracts published by religious associations		free
do wire covered with cotton	15	30 per cent			
Bocking	15		Books, blank, bound or unbound	10	20 per cent
Bodkins, all	15	30 per cent	Books, magazines, pamphlets, periodicals, and all printed matter, illustrated books and papers bound or unbound not otherwise provided for	10	15 per cent
Boiler plates, iron	15	$20 per ton			
Bole, Armenian	10	20 per cent			
Bologna Sausages	15	30 per cent			
Bolting cloths	10	free	Books of engravings, bound or unbound	10	10 per cent
Bolts, composition	15	30 per cent	Books of music bound or unbound	10	10 per cent
do shingle and stave	5	free	Books, specially imported for the use of philosophical and literary societies, schools, churches, &c	free	free
Bonnets	15	30 per cent			
Bonnet-wire covered with silk	15	30 per cent			
Bonnet-wire covered with cotton thread, if wire of chief value	15	30 per cent	Borate of lime	10	10 per cent
Bone alphabets	15	30 per cent	Borax, refined	10	3c per lb
do black	10	free	Borax, crude or tincal	10	free
do chessmen	15	30 per cent	Botany, specimens of	free	free
do whale rosetts	15	30 per cent	Bottles, glass, filled with sweetmeats, or preserves	25	30 per cent
do tip and bones	10	10 per cent	Bottles, apothecaries	15	25 per cent
do whale, other manufactures of	15	30 per cent	do black glass	15	25 per cent
do whale of Amer. fisheries	15	free	do perfumery & fancy	15	30 per cent
do whale not of American fisheries	15	20 per cent			
do manufactures of	15	30 per cent			
Bones burnt and bone dust	10	free			

	U.S.A. Tariff, 1861.	U.S.A. Tariff, 1861.		U.S.A. Tariff, 1861.	U.S.A. Tariff, 1861.
Bottles, cut glass....	25	30 per cent	Brazil pebbles prepared for spectacles..	15	30 per cent
Boug'es	15	8c per lb	Brazil wood,brazilletto and all other dye woods in sticks...	10	free
Boxes, gold or silver.	20	30 per cent	Breccia, in blocks and slabs..........	15	free
Boxes, musical......	15	20 per cent	Brick or fire brick not otherwise provided for..............	15	20 per cent
japanned dressing.	15	30 per cent			
Boxes, cedar, granadilla ebony. rose satin and other woods..........	25	30 per cent	Bricks, burnt or unburnt, of clay.....	10	
Boxes, sand........	15	30 per cent	Brittania ware......	15	30 per cent
do shell...	20	30 per cent	Bridles..............	15	30 per cent
do snuff.........	20	30 per cent	Brimstone, crude....	free	free
do paper and all other fancy boxes.	15	30 per cent	do rolled...	free	20 per cent
Box boards, paper...	15	30 per cent	Bristol boards......	15	30 per cent
do wood unmanuf'd	10	free	do perforated	15	30 per cent
Bracelets, gold or set	25	25 per cent	Bristles............	10	4c per lb
do gilt.....	25	25 per cent	Brodequins, woolen..	15	30 per cent
do hair	20	30 per cent	do leather..	15	30 per cent
Braces and bitts, carpenters'.........	15	30 per cent	Bronze.............	15	
Braces or supenders of India rubber....	15	30 per cent	Bronze casts........	15	30 per cent
Brackets	15	30 per cent	Bronze, manufactures of, or of which bronze is of chief value, not otherwise provided for..	15	30 per cent
Braids, silk....	15	30 per cent			
do hair...	20	30 per cent			
do cotton......	15	20 per cent	Bronze metal in leaf.	10	10 per cent
do in ornaments for head dresses...	15	30 per cent	do powder....	10	20 per cent
Braids, hair, not made up for head dresses	20	25 per cent	Bronze, pale, yellow white and red.....	10	10 per cent
Braids, hair, made up for head dresses...	20	25 per cent	Bronze liquid, gold or bronze color......	10	10 per cent
Braids,straw,for making bonnets or hats	15	30 per cent	Brooms, all kinds....	20	30 per cent
Brandy, first proof..	25	$1 per gal	Brucine (medical preparation).........	15	30 per cent
Brass, manufactures of,or of which brass is the chief value, not otherwise provided for........	15	30 per cent	Brushes, of all kinds.	20	30 per cent
			Buchu leaves.......	10	free
			Buckles.............	15	30 per cent
Brass in plates or sheets..........	10	30 per cent	Bugles, glass, if cut..	25	30 per cent
			do if not cut	15	25 per cent
Brass in bars......	5	10 per cent	Building stones......	10	10 per cent
Brass in pigs.......	5	10 per cent	Bullets.............	free	1½c per lb
Brass, old, only fit to be manufactured..	5	10 per cent	Bulrushes..........		free
Brass, wire........	15	30 per cent	Bulbs..............	10	free
do rolled........	10	30 per cent	Bullion.............	free	free
do battery.... ..	15	30 per cent	Bunting............	15	30 per cent
do studs........	15	30 per cent	Burr stones, wrought or unwrought, not manufactured and not bound up into mill-stones....	10	free
do screws.......	15	30 per cent			
Brazier's rods... ...	15	30 per cent			
Brazil paste, or pasta de Brazil........	10	10 per cent	Burr stones, manufactured or bound up into mill-stones...	10	20 per cent
Brazil pebble.......	5	10 per cent			

	C.S.A. Tariff 1861	U.S.A. Tariff 1861		C.S.A. Tariff 1861	U.S.A. Tariff 1861
Burgundy pitch.....	15	20 per cent	Canes and sticks, walking, finished or not............	20	30 per cent
Busts, lead........	15	30 per cent			
Buttons, all kinds...	15	30 per cent			
Button moulds of whatever material.	15	30 per cent	Cannetille (wire ribbon)............	15	30 per cent
Button cloths......	15	30 per cent	Cannon, brass or iron.	free	30 per cent
Butter...........	10	4c per lb	Cantharides, or Spanish flies..........	10	10 per cent
Butcher's knives....	15	30 per cent			
Butts and hinges, cast iron............	15	2c per lb	Caoutchouc gum (India Rubber)...	10	free
Cabinet wares......	15	30 per cent	Capers............	20	30 per cent
Cabinets of coins for societies, schools, churches, &c.....	free	free	Caps of fur, chip, lace, leather, cotton, silk, linen, &c........	15	30 per cent
Cabinets of coins, metals, gems and all collections of antiquities........	10		Caps, gloves, leggins, mits, socks, stockings, shirts, draws, and all similar articles made on frames, and worn by men, women or children, and not otherwise provided for............	15	30 per cent
Cables, tarred.....	15	2½c per lb			
Cables of whatever material made....	15				
Cables, untarred....	15	3c per lb			
Cables, iron or chain or parts of.......	15	$1.25 per 100 lbs	Cap pieces for stills..	15	30 per cent
Cadmium........	15	free	Caps, lace, sewed or not............	15	30 per cent
Calamine.........	15	free			
Calcined magnesia...	15	30 per cent	Capsules...........	15	30 per cent
Calomel..........	15	20 per cent	Carbines or carabines	free	30 per cent
Camblets, of mohair or goats........	15	30 per cent	Carbonate of magnesia	15	30 per cent
			do of soda....	15	20 per cent
Cameos, real or imitation, not set.	5	5 per cent	do of Ammonia....	10	10 per cent
do set........	10	25 per cent	do of iron....	15	
Camels hair........	10	10 per cent	Carboys...........	15	30 per cent
do pencils ..	15	30 per cent	Carbuncles.........	5	5 per cent
Camphor, refined...	20	6c per lb	Carbuncles set.....	10	25 per cent
do crude.....	10	free	Cardamom seed.....	15	free
Canary seed........	free	free	Card cases.........	20	30 per cent
Canella alba........	10	20 per cent	Cards, playing, visiting, &c..........	20	30 per cent
Candlesticks, alabast'r	25	30 per cent	Carmine...........	15	30 per cent
do glass cut	25	30 per cent	Caroline plaids, cotton and wool........	15	30 per cent
do spar....	25	30 per cent	Carpets and carpeting of Wilton, Saxony, Aubusson, Axminster, patent velvet, and tapestry velvet, Brussels, wrought by the Jacquard machine and all medallion or whole carpets valued at $1.25 or under per square yard.......	15	40c per sq yd
do all other	15	30 per cent			
Candles, tallow.....	15	2c per lb			
do paraffine...	15	4c per lb			
do and tapers, spermaceti or wax	15	8c per lb			
Candles and tapers, spermaceti and wax combined........	15	8c per lb			
Candles and tapers, stearine and all other............	15	4c per lb			
Candy, sugar........	25	4c per lb			

	C.S.A. Tariff, 1861.	U.S.A. Tariff, 1861.		C.S.A. Tariff, 1861.	U.S.A. Tariff, 1861.
Carpets valued at over $1.25 per square yard	15	50c per sq yd	Castors, wood, with or without glass...	15	30 per cent
Carpets, Brussels and Tapestry Brussels.	15	30c per sq yd	Castors, glasses, not in the fra'es, or cruets, cut...	25	30 per cent
Carpets, treble, Ingrain and worsted.	15		Castors, glass, not in the frames or cru'ts, not cut...	15	25 per cent
Carpets, Venetian...	15	25c per sq yd	Castoreum...	15	20 per cent
Carpets, hemp or jute	15	4c per sq yd	Cast shoe bills...	15	30 per cent
Carpets, druggets, bocking and felt, printed colored or otherwise...	15	20c per sq yd	Cast steel in bars....	10	
Carpets, all other kinds, of wool, flax or cotton or parts of either or other materials not otherwise provided for..	15	30 per cent	Cast iron vessels not otherwise specified	15	1c per lb
Carriages and parts of carriages...	15	30 per cent	Catches, brass, copper or iron...	15	30 per cent
Carriage springs....	15	30 per cent	Catechu...	10	free
Carvers...	15	30 per cent	Catgut...	15	20 per cent
Cascarilla...	10	free	Catsup...	20	30 per cent
Cashmere, borders of wool in whole or in part...	15	30 per cent	Caulking mallets....	15	30 per cent
Cashmere gown patterns, wool being a component mat'rial	15	30 per cent	Cedar wood, manufactures of...	25	30 per cent
Cashmere gowns, made...	15	30 per cent	Cedar wood, unmanufactured...	10	free
Cases, fish skin.. ...	15	20 per cent	Cement, Roman.....	15	20 per cent
Cassimere, cotton, wool being a component part, chief value...	15	30 per cent	Cerise, or cher'y wat'r	15	30 per cent
Casks, empty...	15	30 per cent	Chafing dishes...	15	30 per cent
Cassada, or meal of..	15	30 per cent	Chains all sorts.....	15	
Cassia...	10	4c per lb	Chains, trace, halter and fence, of wire rods ¼ inch or over.	15	1¼c per lb
Cassia buds...	10	8c per lb	Chains, under ¼ inch and not under ⅛ in.	15	2c per lb
Castings of plaster or iron, even if with wrought iron rings, hoops, handles, &c.	15	30 per cent	Chains under ⅛ inch and not under No. 9 wire guage....	15	2¼c per lb
Castor beans or seeds	15	10 per cent	Chains under No. 9 wire guage...	15	25 per cent
Castor oil...	15	20 per cent	Chains or cables, iron	15	$1.50 per 100 lbs
Castors, brass, iron or wood...	15	30 per cent	Chains, hair...	20	30 per cent
Castors or cruets, silver, with or without glasses...	20	30 per cent	Chairs, sitting...	15	30 per cent
Castors, cruets, plated with or without glass...	20	30 per cent	Chalk, red, white and French...	10	free
			Chalk, red, pencil...	15	30 per cent
			Chambray, if wool is a component part..	15	30 per cent
			Chambray, of silk only	15	30 per cent
			Chamomile flowers..	15	20 per cent
			Chandeliers, brass..	15	30 per cent
			do glass cut	25	30 per cent
			Charts...	10	free
			Charts, books of, not connected with any work of which they form a volume....	10	free

	C.S.A. Tariff, 1861.	U.S.A. Tariff, 1861.		C.S.A. Tariff, 1861.	U.S.A. Tariff, 1861.
When so connected will pay the same as other volumes..	10	15 per cent	Circassian (worsted)	15	
Charts, for the use of societies, schools, colleges, churches, &c.	free	free	Citrate of lime	15	20 per cent
			Citron in its natural state	10	10 per cent
Cheese	10	4c per lb	Citron preserved	25	30 per cent
Chemical preparations, salts, &c., not otherwise enumerated	15	20 per cent	Civet, oil of	15	30 per cent
			Clasps, all	15	30 per cent
			Clay, ground or prepared	10	
Chenile,cords or trimming, of cotton	15	30 per cent	Clay, unwrought	10	$3 per ton
Cheroots	25	30 per cent	Clay, pipe	10	35c per 100 lbs
Cherry rum	25	50c per gal			
Chessmen, bone,ivory rice or wood	15	30 per cent	Cloaks	15	30 per cent
Chest handles	15	30 per cent	Cloak pins	15	30 per cent
Chicory root	10	20 per cent	Clocks, and parts of clocks	15	30 per cent
do ground	10	20 per cent			
Children's shoes and slippers	15	30 per cent	Cloth, India rubber	15	
China ware of every description	15	10 per cent	Cloth, woolen,wholly or in part of wool	15	12c lb and 25 per cent
China root	15	10 per cent			
Chinchilla skins undressed	5	5 per cent	Cloths, oil, not denominated patent floor cloth	15	30 per cent
Chinchilla skins dressed	15	20 per cent	Cloths and seatings of hair	15	25 per cent
Chip hats or bonnets	15	30 per cent	Cloth, grass	15	25 per cent
Chisels, all	15	30 per cent	Clothing, ready made and wearing apparel, wholly or in part of wool	15	12c per lb and 25 per cent
Chloride of lime	10	10 per cent			
Chlorometers, glass	15	30 per cent	Clothing, ready made not of wool	15	30 per cent
Chocolate	15	20 per cent	Cloves	20	4c per lb
Choppa romals and bandana handkerchiefs, silk	15	30 per cent	Cloves, oil of	15	30 per cent
			Coaches or parts thereof	15	30 per cent
Chromate of potash	15	15 per cent	Coach furniture	15	30 per cent
do lead. :	15	20 per cent	Coal, bituminous	10	$1 per ton
Chrome yellow	15	20 per cent	Coke and culm of coal	10	25 per cent
Chromic acid	10	15 per cent	Coal, all other	10	50c per ton
Chronometers,box or ship and parts thereof	10	10 per cent	ton of 28 bush, 80 lbs to the bush		
			Coal hods	15	30 per cent
Chrysolites	5	20 per cent	Coatings, brown or bleached, of the value of 30 cts and under per sq. yard	15	25 per cent
Ciar, or coiar, rope	15	1c per lb			
Cicuta	15	20 per cent	Coatings, over 30 cts per square yard	15	30 per cent
Cider	15		Cobalt	15	free
Cigars	25	see segars	Cochineal	10	free
do paper	25	30 per cent	Cocculus indicus	10	10 per cent
Cinchona	10	free	Cocks	15	30 per cent
Cinnabar	15	20 per cent	Cocoa, and cocoa leaves	10	free
Cinnamon	20	10c per lb			
Circingle webb (woolen)	15	30 per cent			

15

Item	C.S.A. Tariff, 1861.	U.S.A. Tariff, 1861.
Cocoa, shells	10	free
Cocoa-nuts	10	free
Codilla, or tow of hemp	10	$10 per ton
Codfish, dry	15	50c pr 100 lbs
Coffee, when imported in American vessels, from the place of its growth, &c.	free	free
Coffee, the growth or production of the possessions of the Netherlands, imported from the Netherlands	free	free
Coffee, all other	free	20 per cent
Coffee mills	15	30 per cent
Coins, cabinets of	10	free
Coins, cabinets of for use of societies, schools, churches, &c.	free	free
Coins, gold, silver or copper	free	free
Coir	10	$10 per ton
Coir yarn	10	1c per lb
Coke	10	25 per cent
Cold cream	20	30 per cent
Colocynth	10	free
Collections of antiquities	10	
Collections of antiquities for the use of societies, schools, &c.	free	free
Cologne water	20	30 per cent
Colombo root	15	20 per cent
Coloquintida	10	free
Coloring for brandy	15	30 per cent
Colt's foot	15	20 per cent
Cols, sanglier, cravat stiffeners	15	30 per cent
Combs	15	30 per cent
Commode handles	15	30 per cent
Commode knobs	15	30 per cent
Comforters, made of wool	15	30 per cent
Comfits, preserved in sugar, brandy, or molasses, not otherwise provided for	25	30 per cent
Compasses	15	30 per cent
Composition tops for tables, &c.	25	30 per cent
Composition of glass or paste, set	20	25 per cent

Item	C.S.A. Tariff, 1861.	C.N.A. Tariff, 1861.
Composition of glass or paste, not set	20	10 per cent
Confectionery, all not otherwise provided for	25	30 per cent
Contrayerva root	15	20 per cent
Copper, in pigs, bars, and ingots	5	2c per lb
Copper, old	5	1½c per lb
Copper, braziers and sheets not otherwise provided for	15	25 per cent
Copper bottoms	15	25 per cent
Copper, manufactures of, or which copper is of the chief value not otherwise provided for	15	30 per cent
Copper, for use of the mint	free	free
Copper, sheathing, in sheets 14 inch wide 48 inches long and weighing from 14 to 34 oz the sq foot	5	2c per lb
Copper, rods, bolts, spikes and nails	15	25 per cent
Copper, coins	free	free
Copper, ore	5	5 per cent
Copperas	15	25c pr 100 lbs
Copper, sulphate of	15	20 per cent
Coral, marine	15	free
Coral, cut or manufactured	20	30 per cent
Cordage, tarred	15	2½c per lb
Cordage, untarred manilla	15	2c per lb
Cordage, untarred all others	15	3c per lb
Cordage, vegetable substances, used for cordage	15	$10 per ton
Cordials, all kinds	25	50c per gal
Coriander seed	15	free
Corks	15	20 per cent
Cork tree, manufactures of bark of	15	30 per cent
Cork, bark of unmanufactured	10	free
Cornelian stone	5	5 per cent
Corn fans	15	30 per cent
do Indian or maize	free	10 per bushel
do . meal	free	10 per cent
Corrosive sublimate	15	20 per cent
Corsets	15	30 per cent
Cosmetics	20	30 per cent

Item	U.S.A. Tariff, 1861.	U.S.A. Tariff, 1861.
Cotton.............	free	free
Cotton, linen, silk, wool or worsted, if embroidered or tamboured in the loom or otherwise by machinery or with the needle, or other process not otherwise provided for......	15	30 per cent
Cotton, linen, etc, mixed materials, manufactures, if not otherwise provided for........	15	30 per cent
Cotton, all manufactures of, not bleached, colored, stained or printed, and not over 100 threads to square inch, containing the warp and filling and exceeding 5 oz to the square yard.......	15	1c per sq yd
Cotton do, bleached.	15	1½c per sq yd
Cotton, do, bleached, colored, stained, &c	15	10 pr cent and 1¼c pr sq yd
Cotton, do, not bleached, colored, &c., on finer and lighter goods not over 140 threads to sq inch. &c..............	15	2c per sq yd
Cotton, do, bleached.	15	2¼c per sq yd
Cotton, do, bleached, colored, stained, &c	15	10 pr cent and 2¼c pr sq yd
Cotton, do, not bleached, &c, over 140 threads, and not over 200 threads to square inch, &c...	15	3c per sq yd
Cotton, do, bleached.	15	3½c per sq yd
Cotton, do, bleached, colored and stained, &c..............	15	10 pr cent and 3½c pr sq yd
Cotton do, not bl'ch'd, &c, over 200 thr'ds to square inch.....	15	4c per.sq yd
Cotton, do, bleached.	15	4½c per sq yd
Cotton, do, colored..	15	10 pr cent and 4½c pr sq yd

Item	U.S.A. Tariff, 1861.	U.S.A. Tariff, 1861.
Cotton, goods plain woven and other goods of every description, valued over 16c per square y'd..............	15	25 per cent
Cotton, goods composed of cotton, bleached, unbleached, printed, paint'd or dyed, not otherwise provided for.	15	30 per cent
Cotton shirts and drawers, wove or made on frames, composed wholly of cotton..........	15	25 per cent
Cotton thread.......	15	30 per cent
do lace...........	15	20 per cent
do inserting....	15	20 per cent
do trimming lace.	15	20 per cent
do braids.......	15	20 per cent
do laces, colored.	15	30 per cent
do cords, gimps, and galloons	15	30 per cent
do braces or suspenders....	15	30 per cent
do floss.........	15	30 per cent
Counters, bone, &c..	15	30 per cent
Couting house boxes.	15	30 per cent
Court plaster.......	15	30 per cent
Cowhage down.....	10	20 per cent
Crab-claws........	15	20 per cent
Crackers, fire.......	15	30 per cent
Crapes, silk........	15	30 per cent
Crash, of the value of 30c and under p'r square yard	15	25 per cent
do over 30c per square yard.	15	30 per cent
Cranks, mill, of wr'ht iron........	15	30 per cent
Cravats............	15	30 per cent
Crayons...........	15	30 per cent
Cream of Tartar....	10	free
Crocus powder.....	15	10 per cent
Crockery ware......	15	25 per cent
Crowns, Leghorn hats	15	30 per cent
Crucibles, all.......	15	30 per cent
Cubebs............	15	20 per cent
do oil of.....	15	30 per cent
Cudbear...........	10	free
Cummin seed.......	15	free
Cupboard turns.....	15	30 per cent
Curacoa...........	25	50c per gal
Curls, or ringlets....	20	30 per cent

	C. S. A. Tariff, 1861.	U. S. A. Tariff, 1861.
Currier's knives.....	15	30 per cent
Currants...........	20	2c per lb
Curtain rings.......	15	30 per cent
Custas, as manufactures of cotton....	15	30 per cent
Cutch.............	10	free
Cutlasses..........	free	30 per cent
Cutlery, all kinds...	15	30 per cent
Cyanide of iodine....	15	30 per cent
do potassium..	15	30 per cent
do zinc......	15	30 per cent
Daggers and dirks...	15	30 per cent
Dates.............	20	2c per lb
Decanters, cut......	25	30 per cent
do plain	15	25 per cent
Damasks, valued at 30 cts and under per square yard......	15	25 per cent
Damasks, over 30 cts per square yard...	15	30 per cent
DeLaines, Muslin, Cashmere, and bareges, wholly or in part of wool, and all gray and uncolored goods of similar description	15	25 per cent
Delphinia..........	15	20 per cent
Demijohns.........	15	30 per cent
Denmark satin, or sateens........	15	30 per cent
Dentifrice..........	20	30 per cent
Decoctions and extracts for dyeing..	10	
Diamonds and imitations not set	5	5 per cent
do set........	10	25 per cent
do glaziers' set or not set.	10	10 per cent
Diapers valued at 30c and under per sq yd	15	25 per cent
Diapers valued over 30c per square y'rd	15	30 per cent
Dice, ivory or bone..	15	30 per cent
Distilled vinegar, medicinal.......	15	30 per cent
Diuretic sal........	15	10 per cent
Diva diva.........	15	free
Dolls of every description...........	15	30 per cent
Dominoes, bone or ivory............	15	30 per cent
Doyley's, woolen..	15	30 per cent
Downs, all kinds....	15	20 per cent
Dragons' blood......	10	free
Drawing pencils. ...	15	30 per cent
Drawings..........	10	10 per cent
Drawings for the use of colleges, schools, churches, &c.....	free	free
Drawer knobs of brass iron, steel, ivory, bone washed, gilt or plated.......	15	30 per cent
do of brass & glass..	15	30 per cent
do entirely of cut glass........	25	30 per cent
do entirely of plain glass........	15	25 per cent
Drawing knives.....	15	30 per cent
Drawers, Gurnsey, wool or worsted..	15	30 per cent
do knitted, without needle work..	15	30 per cent
do silk wove......	15	30 per cent
do cotton wove. ...	15	25 per cent
Dried pulp.........	15	20 per cent
Drills and Ducks of the value of 30 cts and under per sq yard...	15	25 per cent
do above 30c per square yard.	15	30 per cent
Drugs, Medicines, not otherwise enumerated, in a crude state............	15	25 per cent
Dutch and bronze metals, in leaf.....	10	10 per cent
Duck, Holland, English, Psnssia, half-duck and all other sail duck........	15	25 per cent
Dust pans........	15	30 per cent
Dye woods and extracts and decoctions of........	10	free
Earth, fuller's......	5	
Earth, brown, red, blue, yellow dry, as ochre...........	15	35c p'r 100 lbs
Earthenware, stone, or crockery-ware, printed, white, glazed, edged, printed, dipped, or cream colored, composed of earthy or mineral substances.......	15	25 per cent
Earthenware, common brown and stoneware........	15	20 per cent

2

Article	C.S.A. Tariff, 1861.	U.S.A. Tariff, 1861.	Article	C.S.A. Tariff, 1861.	U.S.A. Tariff, 1861.
Earthenware, not warranted above the capacity of ten gallons	15	free	Extract of Belladonna	15	30 per cent
Ebony, manufactures of	25	30 per cent	Extract Campeachy wood	10	free
Ebony, unmanufactured	10	free	Etract of cicuta	15	30 per cent
Elastic garters, made of elastic wires, covered with leather, with metal clasps	15	30 per cent	do colocynth	15	30 per cent
			do elaterium	15	30 per cent
			do ergot	16	30 per cent
			do gentian	15	30 per cent
			do hyosciamus	15	30 per cent
Elephant's teeth	10	free	do indigo	10	free
Elecampane	15	20 per cent	do logwood	10	free
Embroideries, all in gold or silver, fine or half fine, or other metal	15	30 per cent	do nux vomica	15	30 per cent
			do madder	10	free
			do opium	15	30 per cent
			do rhatania	15	30 per cent
Embroidery, if done by hand with a needle	15	30 per cent	do rhubarb	15	30 per cent
			do stramonium	15	30 per cent
Emeralds	5	5 per cent	Extracts and decoctions of logwood and other dye w'ods not otherwise provided for	10	free
Emery (in lumps or pulverized)	5	free	Eyes and rods for stairs	15	30 per cent
Emetic, tartar	15	20 per cent	Eyes, balls, glass	15	25 per cent
Enamel, white	15	30 per cent	False collars	15	30 per cent
Encaustic tiles	15	30 per cent	Fans, all	20	30 per cent
Engraver's copper, prepared or polished	15	30 per cent	Fancy or perfumed shaving soaps, including Windsor soaps and wash balls	20	30 per cent
Engraving or plates, bound or unbound	10	10 per cent	Fancy vials & bottles	15	30 per cent
Envelopes, paper	15	30 per cent	Fastenings, shutters or other, of copper, iron brass, steel gilt, plated or japanned	15	30 per cent
Epaulets	20	30 per cent			
Epsom salts	15	20 per cent			
Ergot	10	10 per cent			
do extract of	10		Feathers, ornamental and artificial, and parts thereof	20	30 per cent
Escutcheons, silver, brass, iron, steel, gilt or plated	15	30 per cent	Feathers for beds and feather beds	15	20 per cent
Escutcheon pins	15	30 per cent	Felt, adhesive, for sheathing vessels	5	free
Essences, all	20	30 per cent	Felts, or hat bodies, made in whole or in part of wool	15	20 per cent
Etchings, or engravings	10	10 per cent	Feldspar	15	20 per cent
Etchings for the use of societies, churches, schools, &c	free	free	Felting or blankets, uncolored, for paper or printing machines	15	25 per cent
Ether	15	20 per cent	Felting, hatters	15	30 per cent
Etoil, or stars for ornaments, gold or mislin	15	30 per cent	Fennel, essence of	15	30 per cent
Ether, sulphuric	15	20 per cent			
Extracts for the toilet	20	30 per cent			
Extracts for medicinal purposes	15	30 per cent			

	C.S.A. Tariff, 1861.	U.S.A. Tariff, 1861.		C.S.A. Tariff, 1861.	U.S.A. Tariff, 1861.
Ferri, rubigo	15	10 per cent	Flannels, colored, printed or plaided, or composed in pr't of cotton or silk	15	30 per cent
Fertilizers and manures of all sorts..	free	free			
Fiddles	15	20 per cent	Flap hinges	15	1½c per lb
Fifes, bone, ivory or wood	15	20 per cent	Flasks, or bottles that come in gin cases..	15	30 per cent
Figures, alabaster	25	30 per cent	Flasks, powder, brass, copper, japanned or horn	15	30 per cent
do other	15	30 per cent			
Figs	20	3c per lb			
Filberts	10	1c per lb			
Fig, blue	15	20 per cent	Flat irons	15	30 per cent
File cuts	15	30 per cent	Flats for making hats or bonnets	15	30 per cent
Files	15	30 per cent			
Fire arms and all parts thereof not intended for military purposes	15		Flax unmanufactured	10	$15 per ton
			Flax manufactures of not otherwise specified	15	30 per cent
Fire works, all kinds.	15		Flaxseed	10	10c per bush'l of 52 lbs
Fire crackers	15	30 per cent			
do screens	20	30 per cent	Fleams	15	30 per cent
do wood		20 per cent	Fleshers	15	30 per cent
Fish, (foreign caught) other than in bar'ls, or half bar'ls, fresh, smoked, dried, salted or pickled, not otherwise provided for	15	50c pr 100 lbs	Flies, Spanish or cantharides	10	10 per cent
			Flints	10	free
			Flint stone	10	free
			do ground	10	free
			Float files	15	30 per cent
Fish, herrings, pickl'd or salted	15	$1 per barrel	Flocks	10	10 per cent
			Flocks, waste or shoddy	10	
do mackerel	15	$2 per barrel	Floor cloth, oiled, stamped, painted or printed valued at 50c or less per sq yd	15	20 per cent
do salmon, pickled	15	$3 per barrel			
do preserved in oil	25	30 per cent			
do prepared	15	30 per cent	Floor cloths, do, over 50c per sq yard.	15	30 per cent
Fish, pickled, all oth'rs not otherwise provided for in barrels	15	$1.50 per bbl	do all others	15	30 per cent
Fish glue, or isinglass	15	20 per cent	Floor cloths, lined with woolen or wool	15	30 per cent
do hooks	15	30 per cent	Flor. Benzoin	15	30 per cent
do sauce	15	30 per cent	Florentine buttons, covered with bombazette over a met'l form	15	30 per cent
do skins	15	20 per cent			
do skin cases	15	20 per cent			
Fish, fresh, caught for daily consumption.	15	free	Floss silk, and other similar silks, purified from the gum.	15	20 per cent
Fisheries of the U.S. and their territories all products of	15	free	Floss cotton	15	30 per cent
Fishing nets	15	30 per cent	Flour, of wheat	free	10 per cent
do lines	15	30 per cent	do of rye	free	10 per cent
Flageolets, wood, bone or ivory	15	20 per cent	do of sulphur	10	20 per cent
Flannels, valued at 30 cts or less pr sq yd.	15	25 per cent	Flower water, orange	15	30 per cent
Flannels, valued over 30c per sq yard	15	30 per cent	Flowers, artificial or ornamental	20	30 per cent

Article	C.S.A. Tariff 1861	U.S.A. Tariff 1861
Flowers used in dyeing in a crude state	5	free
Flowers, chamomile	15	20 per cent
Flues of wrought iron	15	2c per lb
Flutes of wood, ivory or bone	15	20 per cent
Flushings	15	30 per cent
Foils, fencing	15	30 per cent
Foil, copper	15	30 per cent
Foil, silver	20	20 per cent
Foil, tin	10	10 per cent
Fol. digitalis	15	20 per cent
Forks, all	15	30 per cent
Forge hammers	15	30 per cent
Fossils	10	free
Fowls, land & water	free	free
Foxglove	15	20 per cent
Frames, or sticks for umbrellas, parasols and sun-shades	15	30 per cent
Frames, plated cruets	15	30 per cent
do quadrant	15	30 per cent
do silver cruet	20	30 per cent
Frankfort black	15	20 per cent
Frankincense, a gum	15	free
French chalk	10	
Fringes, cotton	15	see cotton
do wool	15	30 per cent
do silk	15	30 per cent
Frizettes, hair	20	30 per cent
Frocks, Guernsey	15	30 per cent
Fruits, West India, in their natural state	10	
Fruits, preserved in sugar, brandy, or molasses, not otherwise provided for	25	30 per cent
Fruits, preserved in own juice	15	20 per cent
do pickled	15	30 per cent
do prepared	20	30 per cent
do juices of, with sugar	10	
Frying pans	15	30 per cent
Fuller's boards	15	30 per cent
Fuller's earth	5	free
Fulminates, or fulminating powders	15	20 per cent
Furniture and household effects of persons or families fr'm foreign countries if used abroad by them and not intended for sale	free	
Furniture, coach and harness	15	30 per cent
Furniture, brass, copper, iron or steel, not coach or harness	15	30 per cent
Furniture, cabinet and household	15	30 per cent
Furniture, calico or chintz	15	30 per cent
Furs, undressed, on the skin	10	10 per cent
Fur, dressed, on the skin	15	10 per cent
Furs, dressed or undressed not on the skin	10	
Furs, hats or caps of	15	30 per cent
do hat bodies or felts	15	30 per cent
do hatters', dressed or undressed	10	10 per cent
Fur muffs or tippets, and all other manufactures of fur, or of which fur is a component mat'rial	15	30 per cent
Galangal, or Galangal root	15	20 per cent
Galoons, gold and silver	20	30 per cent
do silk or cotton	15	30 per cent
Galls, nut	10	free
Gambia, (Terra. Japonica)	10	free
Gamboge	10	10 per cent
Game bags, leather or twine	15	30 per cent
Game, prepared	20	30 per cent
Garance, or madder	10	free
Garnets and imitations	5	5 per cent
Garnets set	10	25 per cent
Garden seed and all other seeds for agricultural & horticultural purposes	free	free
Garancine, extract of madder	10	free
Garters, India Rubber with clasps	15	30 per cent
Gas retorts, clay	10	
Gelatine	15	30 per cent
Gems, or imitations not set	5	5 per cent
Gems, set	10	25 per cent

Article	C.S.A. Tariff, 1861.	U.S.A. Tariff, 1861.
Gems, collections of, for use of societies, schools, &c	free	free
Gems, cabinets of	10	
Gentian, or gentian root	15	20 per cent
German silver	20	30 per cent
Gig hames, springs, or handles	15	30 per cent
Gilt fancy ware, wire, &c	20	30 per cent
Gimlets	15	30 per cent
Gimps, cotton	15	30 per cent
Gimps, wire being a component part	15	30 per cent
Gin, (first proof)	25	40c per gal
Ginger root	15	free
do green	15	
Ginger, ground, preserved or pickled	15	10 per cent
Gin cases, with bottles	25	30 per cent
Ginghams	15	see cotton
Ginseng	15	20 per cent
Glass of antimony	15	20 per cent
Glass bottles or jars filled with sweetmeats, preserves, or other articles		30 per cent
Glass, cut, manuf. of	25	30 per cent
Glass, engraved, col'd, painted, stained, silvered or gilded	15	30 per cent
Glass, plain, moulded or pressed, not cut, engrav'd or paint'd	15	25 per cent
Glass rough plate, cylinder, or broad window n't exceeding 10x15 in	15	1c pr sq foot
" Over the above and not exceeding 16 by 24	15	1½c pr sq ft
" Over the above and not exceed'g 24x30	15	2c per sq ft
" Over the above and not exceeding in weight 1 lb pr sq ft	15	3c per sq ft
" All over the above	15	add on excess at same rate
Glass, crown, plate or polished & all other window glass not exceeding 10x15 in.	15	1½c pr sq ft
" Above, and not exceeding 16x24 inch	15	2½c pr sq ft
Glass Above, and not exceeding 24x30 in	15	4c pr sq ft
" All above	15	5c pr sq ft
" Weighing over 150 lbs per 100 sq feet additional duty on such excess of		4c per lb
" Porcelain and Bohemian	15	30 per cent
" Crystals for watch's	15	30 per cent
" paintings	20	30 per cent
" or pebbles for spectacles	15	30 per cent
" plates or disks unwrought for optical instruments	15	10 per cent
" articles n't specifi'd connected with other materials not otherwise provided for	15	30 per cent
" when old, not in pieces which can be cut for use, and fit only to be remanufactured	10	free
" manufactures of, all vessels and wares not otherwise provided for	15	30 per cent
" green, pocket bottles	15	25 per cent
" looking, plates, silvered	15	30 per cent
Glasses, hour	15	30 per cent
Glasses, looking	15	30 per cent
Glauber salts	15	20 per cent
Glaziers' diamonds	10	10 per cent
Gloves	15	30 per cent
Glue	15	20 per cent
Goats' skins, raw	5	5 per cent
do tanned	10	20 per cent
Goats' hair not provided for	10	
Gold, bullion	free	free
Gold, manufactures of, or of which gold is of chief value, not otherwise provided for	20	30 per cent
Gold beater's skins	10	10 per cent
do dust	free	free
do embroideries	20	30 per cent
do leaf	10	20 per cent
do muriate of	15	30 per cent
do oxide of	15	30 per cent

	C.S.A. Tariff, 1861.	U.S.A. Tariff, 1861.
Gold paper, in sheets, strips, or other forms	15	30 per cent
do size	15	20 per cent
do shell for paint'g	15	30 per cent
do studs	20	25 per cent
Golo shoes or clogs..	15	30 per cent
Gouges	15	30 per cent
Gowns	15	30 per cent
Gown patterns, wool being a component part	15	30 per cent
Grains of Paradise...	10	free
Granadilla wood, manufactures of...	25	30 per cent
Granadilla wood unmanufactured	10	free
Grapes	20	20 per cent
Grass bags	15	30 per cent
do cloth	15	25 per cent
do flats, braids or plaits	15	30 per cent
do hats or bonnets	15	30 per cent
Grasshopper springs.	15	30 per cent
Grass, Sisal	10	$10 per ton
Grass, Sisal, or Jute, all manufactures of, not otherwise provided for	15	20 per cent
Grease	10	10 per cent
Green, French, mineral and olympian...	15	20 per cent
Green turtle	15	10 per cent
Gridirons	15	30 per cent
Grindstones, wrought or finished	10	10 per cent
Grindstones, unfinished	10	free
Guava jelly, or paste.	25	30 per cent
Guernsey frocks	15	30 per cent
Gunny bags	15	2c per sq yd
Guano	free	free
Guano, imitation of..	free	free
Guinea grains	10	free
Guitars	15	20 per cent
Guitar strings, gut...	15	20 per cent
Gum copal	10	10 per cent
Gum purdu, as opium	15	$1 per lb
Gum substitute or burnt starch	10	10 per cent
Gum, Senegal, Arabic and Tragacanth, Barbary, East India & Jedda myrrh and all other gums and resins, in a crude state, not otherwise provided for	10	free
Gum, elastic articles.	15	30 per cent
Gum, benzoin or benjamin	15	
Guns, except muskets and rifles	15	30 per cent
Gunpowder	free	20 per cent
Gunny cloth	15	2c per sq yd
Gutta percha unmn'nufactured	5	free
Guta percha, manufactures of	15	20 per cent
Gypsum	5	free
Hackles, all kinds...	15	30 per cent
Hair, made up for head dresses	20	25 per cent
Hair, of all kinds, uncleansed and unmanufactured, and all long horse hair, used for weaving, cleaned or uncleaned, drawn or undrawn	10	free
Hair, of alpaca, goat and other like animals, unmanufactured	10	
Hair, manufactures of, goat's hair or mohair not otherwise provided for	15	30 per cent
Hair nets	15	25 per cent
Hair cloth and seatings, and all other manufactures of hair not otherwise provided for	15	25 per cent
Hair, curled, moss, sea-weed, and all other vegetable substances used for beds or mattings..	15	20 per cent
Hair, braids for the head	20	30 per cent
Hair, belts & brooms	15	30 per cent
Hair, bracelets, chains, ringlets and curls..	20	30 per cent
Hair of all kinds, cleansed, but unmanufactured, not		

	C. S. A. Tariff, 1861.	U. S. A. Tariff, 1861.		C. S. A. Tariff, 1861.	U. S. A. Tariff, 1861.
otherwise provided for.............	10	10 per cent	Hatter's irons.......	15	1c per lb
Hair gloves........	15	25 per cent	Hautboys..........	15	20 per cent
Hair, human, prepared and cleaned for use.............	20	30 per cent	Haversacks,of leather	15	30 per cent
			Hayknives.........	15	30 per cent
			Head pieces for stills.	15	30 per cent
Hair pins..........	15	30 per cent	Hearth rugs, all.....	15	30 per cent
Hair powder, per-fumed...........	20	30 per cent	Hellebore root......	15	20 per cent
			Hemlock seed......	15	free
Hair powder, not per-fumed............	20	20 per cent	Hemp seed.........	10	10c pr bush of 52 lbs
Hair pencils.........	15	30 per cent	Hemp, all manuf's of, not oth'rwise speci-fied, or of which hemp is a compon-ent material, not otherwise provided for.............	15	20 per cent
Hames, wood.......	15	30 per cent			
Hammers and sledges, blacksmith's......	15	2c per lb			
Hams and bacon....	free	2c per lb			
Hand-barrows or p'rts of.............	15		Hemp, unmanufactu'd	10	$35 per ton
Handkerchiefs, linen, of the value of 30c or under per sq yd.	15	25 per cent	Hemp, manilla and other hemps of In-dia............	10	$15 per ton
Handkerchiefs, do, of the value of over 30 cts per sq yard....	15	30 per cent	Hemp, sun.........		$10 per ton
			Herrings, pickled or salted...........	15	$1 per bbl
Handkerchiefs, cotton	15	(see cotton)	Hides, raw,dried,salt ed or pickled, not otherwise provided for.............	5	5 per cent
Handkerchiefs, silk..	15	30 per cent			
Handles for chests...	15	30 per cent			
Hangers...........	15	30 per cent	Hides, tanned......	10	20 per cent
Hangings, paper.....	15	30 per cent	Hinges, wrought iron	15	1¼c per lb
Hares' hair or fur....	10	10 per cent	Hobby horses.......	15	30 per cent
Hare skins, dressed..	10	10 per cent	Hods..............	15	30 per cent
Hare skins, undressed	5	10 per cent	Hoes..............	15	30 per cent
Harlaem oil........	15	30 per cent	Hollands, brown, of the value of 30c or under per sq yard.	15	25 per cent
Harness...........	15	30 per cent			
Harness furniture....	15	30 per cent	Hollands, if over 30c to sq yard.......	15	30 per cent
Harp strings, gut....	15	20 per cent	Hollow ware, glazed or tinned........	15	2½c per lb
Harp strings, wire...	15	30 per cent			
Harps and harpis-chords..........	15	20 per cent	Hones.............	15	20 per cent
Hartshorn..........	10	30 per cent	Honey.............	15	10c per gal
Hatchets..........	15	30 per cent	Hooks, all.........	15	30 per cent
Hat bodies of wool, or of which wool is a component ma-terial of chief value	15	20 per cent	Hooks and eyes.....	15	30 per cent
			Hops.............	10	10 per cent
Hat bodies, cotton...	15	30 per cent	Horn, manufactures of...............	15	30 per cent
Hats and bonnets for men, women and children, of straw, chip, grass, palm-leaf, willow, hair, whalebone, &c., not otherwise provided for..............	15	30 per cent	Horn combs.......	15	30 per cent
			Horn tips.........	10	10 per cent
			Honru, plates for lan-terns............	15	10 per cent
			Horses...........	free	10 per cent
Hats of wool.......	15	20 per cent	Household furniture..	15	30 per cent
Hats of fur..........	15		Hosiery, cotton, on frames...........	15	20 per cent

Item	U.S.A. Tariff, 1861.	U.S.A. Tariff, 1861.
Household effects, in use when travelling abroad or of persons fr'm fo'gn countries	free	free
Huckabacks, of the value of 30 cts and under per square yard	15	25 per cent
Huckabacks of the value of over 30 cts per square yard	15	30 per cent
Hungary water	20	30 per cent
Hyacinth roots	10	free
Hydriodate of potash	15	15 per cent
Hydrometers of glass	15	30 per cent
Ice, per ton	$1½	free
Imitation of precious stones		5 per cent
Imitation of precious stones not set	5	
Imitation of precious stones set	10	
Instruments, Dental, Mathematical, Surgical, &c	15	
India hemp	10	$15 per ton
India rubber, in bottles	5	
India rubber in slabs or sheets, unmanufactured	5	free
India rubber, milk of	5	free
" " boots and shoes, or other manufactured articles, composed wholly of India rubber, not otherwise provided	15	... per cent
India rubber suspenders, braces, webbing, or other fabrics compos'd wholly or in part of India rubber, not otherwise provided for	15	30 per cent
Indian corn, or maize	free	10c per bush.
" meal	free	10 per cent
Indigo	5	free
Indispensables, bags or leather	15	30 per cent
Indispensables, Merino stuff	15	30 per cent
Indispensables, silk	15	30 per cent
Ink	15	30 per cent
Ink powder	15	30 per cent
Ink stands	15	30 per cent
" " glass, cut	25	30 per cent
Iridium	15	free
Ins'ments for schools, &c	free	free
Instruments, musical	15	20 per cent
Inventions, models of	free	free
Iodine	15	15 per cent
Iodine, salts of	15	15 per cent
Iodine, crude	15	10 per cent
Iodine, resublimed	15	15 per cent
Ipecac. or ipecacuanha	15	10 per cent
India bagging and matting of all sorts not otherwise provided for	15	
Iris root	15	free
Iron, manufactures of, or of which iron is of chief value, not otherwise provided for	15	30 per cent
Iron taggers	15	10 per cent
Iron castings, not otherwise provided for	15	25 per cent
Iron liquor	15	10 per cent
Iron, bar, rolled or hammered	15	$15 per ton
Iron for railroads	15	$12 per ton
Iron boiler plates	15	$20 per ton
Iron, all other rolled and hammered	15	$20 per ton
Iron tire for locomotives or any parts thereof	15	1½ cts per lb.
Iron, in pigs	10	$6 per ton
Iron vessels, cast, not otherwise provided for	15	1 ct per lb
Iron pipes, cast	15	5c. per 100 lbs
Iron castings not otherwise provided for	15	25 per cent
Iron, old scraps	10	$6 per ton
Iron ore	10	
Iron, band and hoop	15	$20 per ton
Iron, slit rod, for nails, nuts, and horseshoes, not otherwise provided for	15	$20 per ton
Iron, maleable in castings, not otherwise provided for	15	2 cts per lb
Iron sheet, smooth, or polished	15	2 cts per lb

Article	C.S.A. Tariff, 1861	U.S.A. Tariff, 1861
Iron, other sheet iron, not thinner than No. 20 wire gauge.	15	$20 per ton
Iron, sheet, thinner than 20 and not thinner than No. 25	15	$25 per ton
Iron, sheet, thinner than 25	15	$30 per ton
Iron, mill irons, and mill cranks of wrought iron, and wrought iron for ships, locomotives, and steam engines, or parts thereof, weighing each 25 lbs, or more	15	1½ cts per lb
Iron galvanized, or iron coated with zinc	15	2 cts per lb
Iron loops	10	
Iron, sulphate of	15	
Isinglass	15	30 per cent
Issue Peas	15	30 per cent
Issue plaster	15	30 per cent
Ivory	10	free
Ivory, manufactures of	15	30 per cent
Ivory, black	15	free
Ivory nuts or vegetable ivory	10	free
Ivory, unmanufact'd	10	free
Ivory vegetable, manufactures of	15	30 per cent
Jacks, for piano fortes	15	30 per cent
Jacks, clothiers'	15	30 per cent
Jacks, chains and screws	15	30 per cent
Jalap	15	10 per cent
Japanned wares, all kinds	15	30 per cent
Jellies, and all other similar preparations	25	30 per cent
Jerked beef	free	1ct per lb
Jet, and manufactures of, real or composition	15	30 per cent
Jewelry	15	25 per cent
Jewelry false, so call'd	15	20 per cent
Juice of oranges, &c.	10	10 per cent
Juniper berries	15	10 per cent
Juniper plants	10	free
Junk, old	5	free
Jute	10	$10 per ton
Jute carpeting		40c per sqr yd
Jute, Sisal grass unmanufactured	10	
Jute yarn	15	4 cts per lb
Jute goods	15	15 per cent
Jute or sisal grass, all manufactures of, not otherwise provided for	15	20 per cent
Jute butts	15	$5 per ton
Kaleidoscopes	15	30 per cent
Kalydor	20	30 per cent
Kelp	10	free
Kermes	10	free
Kermes, mineral	10	10 per cent
Kerosine, and all other coal oil	15	10 cts per gal
Kerseys	15	
Kettles, brass	15	30 per cent
Kettles, copper	15	30 per cent
Keys, watch, gold or silver	20	30 per cent
Keys, all other of iron brass, copper, &c.	15	30 per cent
Kilmarnock caps	15	30 per cent
Kirschenwasser	25	50 cts per gal
Knitting needles	15	20 per cent
Knives, all, of iron, steel, copper, brass, pewter, lead or tin.	15	30 per cent
Knobs, brass, iron, steel, copper or brass	15	30 per cent
Knobs, gilt, plated or washed	20	30 per cent
Knobs, cut glass	25	30 per cent
Knobs, glass, not cut.	15	20 per cent
Knobs, glass with brass, iron, steel, or composition shanks	15	30 per cent
Knots of gold, silver.	20	30 per cent
Kreosote	15	30 per cent
Labels, printed	15	30 per cent
Labels, gilt or plated	20	30 per cent
Labels, gold or silver	20	30 per cent
Lac dye		10 free
Lac spirits		10 free
Lac sulphur		10 free
Lace, of all kinds, made into wearing apparel	15	30 per cent
do bobbinet	15	30 per cent
do shawls, if sewed	15	30 per cent
do bobbinet veils, cotton	15	30 per cent
Laces, silk	15	30 per cent
do cotton	15	20 per cent
do colored	15	30 per cent

	C.S.A. Tariff, 1861.	U.S.A. Tariff, 1861.		C.S.A. Tariff, 1861.	U.S.A. Tariff, 1861.
do thread and inserting....	15	20 per cent	Lavender water.....	20	30 per cent
do gold, silver, &c.	20	30 per cent	Lawns, cotton......	15	see cotton
Laced boots and bootees..........	15	30 per cent	Lawns, linen of the value of 30 cts or under per sqr yard	15	25 per cent
Ladles, iron, tin, Britania, brass, copper, or gilt	15	30 per cent	Lawns, valued over 30 cts per square yard	15	30 per cent
Ladles heads.......	15	30 per cent	Lawns, or long lawn, linen............	15	see linen
Lake (water colors)..	15	30 per cent	Lead, manufactures of, or of which lead is of chief value, not otherwise provided for........	15	30 per cent
Lake drop colors....	15	30 per cent	Lead, busts.........	15	30 per cent
Lamp black........	15	20 per cent	" in bars........	free	1 ct per lb
Lamp hooks or pulleys, brass, copper, iron, or wood.....	15	30 per cent	" black or plumbago..........	15	10 per cent
Lamps, brass, copper, tin	15	30 per cent	" combs.........	15	30 per cent
Lamps, cut glass.....	25	30 per cent	" old	free	1 ct per lb
Lamps, with brass pillars and glass chimneys, or domes, imported in them....	15	30 per cent	" in pigs	free	1 ct per lb
Lancets	15	30 per cent	" scrap	free	1 ct per lb
do cases, shagreen paper or leather..	15	30 per cent	" sugar of.......	15	3 cts per lb
Lantern leaves, or horn plates......	15	10 per cent	" pots, black.....	15	30 per cent
Lanterns, jappanned, tin, gilt, plated, brass, pewter, or copper..........	15	30 per cent	" nitrate of......	15	3 cts per lb
Lard	free	2 cts per lb	" in sheets	15	1½ cts per lb
Larding pins........	15	30 per cent	" shot..........	15	1¼ct per lb
Lastings, moh'ir cloth, silk, twist, or other manufactures of cloth, in strips, or patterns of the size and shape for buttons, slippers, boots, gaiters, shoes or bootees exclusively not combined with India rubber......	15	free	" shot for cannon, muskets, rifles or pistols.....	free	1½ cts per lb
Do. do. do., of whatever material composed	15		" toys	15	30 per cent
Latches, iron, brass, steel, or copper...	15	30 per cent	" pipe	15	1½ cts per lb
Latches, gilt, plated, or washed........	20	30 per cent	" ore	10	1 ct per lb
Lathes	10	20 per cent	" pencils........	15	30 per cent
Lattin, brass........	15	30 per cent	" in any other form not specified..	15	30 per cent
Laudanum	15	30 per cent	Leaders, leather.....	15	30 per cent
Lavender, dry flowers of..............	15	20 per cent	Leaf, gold and silver..	10	20 per cent
			" tobacco, unmanufactured.	10	
			Leather bracelets, elastic	15	30 per cent
			Leather mitts	15	30 per cent
			do garters, elastic	15	30 per cent
			do man'fact'r's of, or of which leather is a component part not otherwise provided for....	15	30 per cent
			do upper, of all kinds except calf skins...	10	20 per cent
			do calf skins tanned........	10	25 per cent

	C.S.A. Tariff, 1861.	U.S.A. Tariff, 1861.		C.S.A. Tariff, 1861.	U.S.A. Tariff, 1861.
do patent, or japanned	15	30 per cent	Linens, do, if over 30 cts per square yard	15	30 per cent
do tanned,bend or sole	10	20 per cent	Linen mitts	15	30 per cent
Leaves, medicinal in a crude state	15	20 per cent	Linen tape	15	20 per cent
Leaves for dyeing in a crude state	10	free	Links, coat	15	30 per cent
Leaves not used in dyeing, not otherwise provided for..	15	20 per cent	Linseed	10	10c per bush
Leaves, buchu	15	free	Linseed cake or meal	free	20 per cent
do palm	15	free	Linsey woolsey	15	30 per cent
Leeches	15	free	Lint	15	20 per cent
Lees, wine, liquid...	15		Liquors, spirituous, not enumerated	25	33¼ per cent
Leghorn hats or bonnets, and all hats or bonnets of straw, chip or grass	15	30 per cent	Liquor bronze	10	10 per cent
Leghorn flats, braids, crowns or plaits..	15	30 per cent	do iron	15	10 per cent
Lemons, in bulk, in boxes, barrels or cases	10	10 per cent	do purple	10	10 per cent
Lemon and lime juice	10	10 per cent	do tin	10	10 per cent
Lemon peel	15	10 per cent	do cases	15	30 per cent
Leno, linen	15	(see linen)	Liquorice paste or juice	15	3c per lb
Leno, muslin	15	(see cotton)	Liquorice root	15	free
Leopard skins, raw..	5	5 per cent	Litharge	15	1¼c per lb
Leopard skins, dress'd	15	20 per cent	Lithographic stones..	15	20 per cent
Leopard spot cloth..	15	30 per cent	Lithontriptons	15	30 per cent
Lignumvitæ,unmanufactured	10	free	Litmus	10	free
Limes and lime juice.	10	10 per cent	Loadstones	15	30 per cent
Lime	10	10 per cent	Lotions, all cosmetic.	20	30 per cent
Lime, borate of	10	10 per cent	Lozenges, all medicinal	15	30 per cent
Lime, chloride of	10	15c pr 100 lbs	Locks, all	15	30 per cent
Lines, fishing	15	30 per cent	Longcloths, linen	15	(see linen)
Lines, worsted	15	30 per cent	Looking-glasses,pl'tes or frames	15	30 per cent
Linens, brown or bleached, ducks, canvass paddings, cot bottoms,burlaps drills, coatings, brown Hollands, blay linens, damasks, diapers,crash, huckabacks, lawns, or other manufactures of flax, jute or hemp, or of which flax, jute or hemp shall be the material of chief value, of the value of 30c or under per sq yard..	15	25 per cent	Lunar caustic	15	30 per cent
			Lumber, sawed	10	
			Lustres, glass, cut. ..	25	30 per cent
			Lustres, brass & glass	15	30 per cent
			Lutes	15	20 per cent
			Ley, soda	10	10 per cent
			Macaroni	15	30 per cent
			Mace	20	15c per lb
			Mackerel	15	$2 per bbl
			Machinery of every description, not otherwise provided for	15	
			Machinery, models of & other inventions.	free	free
			Machinery exclusively imported for the manufacture of flax and linen goods...	15	free
			Madder, ground or prepared	10	free
			Madder root	10	free
			Madder, extract of...	10	free
			Madras handkerchiefs cotton	15	30 per cent

	C.S.A. Tariff, 1861.	U.S.A. Tariff, 1861.
Magazines & periodicals............	10	
Magic lanterns......	15	30 per cent
Magnesia.........	15	20 per cent
do carbonate of	15,30 per cent	
do sulphate of.	15,20 per cent	
Mahogany..........	10	free
do manuf. of.	25	30 per cent
Mallets, wood......	15	30 per cent
Malt......	15	20 per cent
Manganese..........	15	10 per cent
Manilla and other hemps of India....	10	$15 per ton
Manna.............	15	10 per cent
Mantillas, silk......	15,30 per cent	
Mantles..........	15	30 per cent
Manufactures of cedar wood, granadilla, ebony, mahogany, rosewood satin-wood...........	25	30 per cent
Manufactures of gold, platina, or silver, not otherwise provided for........	20	
Manufactures not otherwise provided for, composed of mixed materials, in part of cotton, silk, wool, worsted or flax.............	15	30 per cent
Manufact. of Mohair cloth, silk, twist, or manufact. of cloth, suitable for the manufact. of shoes, in strips or patterns of the size and shape for buttons, shoes, or bootees, exclusively, not combined with India rubber......	15	free
Manures & fertilizers of all sorts........	free	free
Maps and charts.....	10	free
Maps and charts for the use of societies, colleges, churches, schools, &c........	free	free
Maraschino..........	25	50c per gal
Marble, saw'd, dress'd, squar'd or polished, manufactures of	15	30 per cent
Marble in the rough		

	C.S.A. Tariff, 1861.	U.S.A. Tariff, 1861.
or blocks.........	10	30 per cent
Marble, toys, baked or stones..........	15	30 per cent
Marble table tops....	15	30 per cent
Marine coral, unmanufactured.........	5	free
Marmalade, a sweet-meat...........	25,30 per cent	
Marrow, and all other grease and soap stocks and soap stuffs.............	10	10 per cent
Marsh mallows......	15	20 per cent
Mastic..............	10	
Matches for pocket lights...........	15	30 per cent
Mathematical instruments imported for any college, academy, school, &c....	free	free
Mathematical instruments...........	15	30 per cent
Mats, cocoa nut.....	15	20 per cent
do table, straw, tow or flag......	15	30 per cent
do table, wool.....	15	30 per cent
do sheepskin....	15	30 per cent
do oil, or floorcloth	15	
do dish or table...	15	30 per cent
Matting, cocoa nut...	15	20 per cent
do all floor, of flags, jute or grass......	15	20 per cent
do China and other floor..	15	20 per cent
Mats, screens, hassocks, and rugs, and all others not specified............	15	30 per cent
Mattrasses, hair or moss, linen tick...	15	20 per cent
Meal, corn..........	free	10 per cent
Meal, oat..........	free	10 per cent
Meats, prepared.....	20	30 per cent
Medals and other antiquities............	10	free
Medals of gold, and silver............	20	free
Medicinal preparations not otherwise provided for......	15	30 per cent
Medicinal roots and leaves and other drugs & medicines in a crude state, not otherwise specified	15	20 per cent

29

Article	C.S.A. Tariff, 1861.	U.S.A. Tariff, 1861.	Article	C.S.A. Tariff, 1861.	U.S.A. Tariff, 1861.
Metal, silver-plated..	20	30 per cent	Mohair, manuf. of, or of which mohair is of chief value, not otherwise provided for	15	30 per cent
Metallic slates, paper or tin	15	30 per cent	Mohair, unmanuf., not provided for	10	
Metallic pens	15	30 per cent	Molasses	20	2 cts per gal.
Metals, unmanufact., not otherwise provided for	10	20 per cent	Moon knives	15	30 per cent
Melting or glue pots, earthen	15	30 per cent	Mops	15	30 per cent
Mercury, or quicksilver	15	10 per cent	Morocco skins	15	20 per cent
Mercury, all preparations of	15	20 per cent	Morphine, and its salts	15	$1 per oz.
Merino shawls, body, of worsted or combed wool	15	30 per cent	Mortars, brass, marble, or composition	15	30 per cent
Merino shawls, bord'r of woolen fringe sewed on	15	30 per cent	Moss, Iceland	10	10 per cent
Merino cloth, entirely of combed wool	15	30 per cent	do for beds	15	20 per cent
Merino cloth, wool not combed being a component part	15	30 per cent	Mosaics, real and imitation not set	5	5 per cent
Merino fringe, worst'd	15	(see wool)	do do set	10	25 per cent
Merino trimmings	15		Mother of pearl	10	free
Merino shawls, made of wool	15	30 per cent	do of pearl articles made of, not otherwise enumerated	15	30 per cent
Manilla hemp	10	$15 per ton	Mother of pearl studs	15	25 per cent
Mica, isinglass	10	20 per cent	do of pearl, buttons with metal eyes or shanks	15	30 per cent
Military accoutrements	free		Moulds, button	15	30 per cent
Milk of roses	20	30 per cent	Mouse traps, wood or wire	15	30 per cent
Millepedes		20 per cent	Muffs, of fur	15	30 per cent
Mill saws	15	30 per cent	Munjeet, or India madder	10	free
Mills, coffee	15	30 per cent	Munitions of war	free	
Millinery of all kinds	15	30 per cent	Muriate of barytes, tin, or strontium	15	20 per cent
Miniature cases, ivory	15	30 per cent	Music in sheets or bound	10	10 per cent
Miniature sheet, ivory	15	30 per cent	Music paper	15	10 per cent
Miniatures	10	free	Musical instruments, all kinds	15	20 per cent
Mineralogy, specim'ns of	free	free	Musical instrument strings of all kinds, of whip-gut or cat-gut, part of metal	15	30 per cent
Mineral and bituminous substances, in a crude state not otherwise provided for	10	20 per cent	Mushrooms	free	30 per cent
Mineral waters	15	30 per cent	Mushroom sauce	15	30 per cent
Mineral blue	15	free	Musk	15	30 per cent
Mineral kermes	10	free	Muskets, rifles, and other fire arms for military purposes	free	30 per cent
Mock pearls	5	5 per cent			
Models of invention, or improvement, not fitted for use	free	free			

Article	U.S.A. Tariff 1861	U.S.A. Tariff 1861	Article	U.S.A. Tariff 1861	U.S.A. Tariff 1861
Musket bayonets....	free	30 per cent	Nitrous acid........	10	10 per cent
do barrels.....	free	30 per cent	Norfolk latches......	15	30 per cent
do bullets]....	free	1½ cts per lb.	Noyeau...........	25	50 cts per gal.
do rods or stocks....	free	30 per cent	Nutria skins, if un. dressed..........	5	5 per cent
Mustard, ground or manuf......	15	20 per cent	Nutgalls...........	10	free
do seed........	15	free	Nutmegs...........	20	15 cts per lb.
Myrrh, in a crude state......	10	free	Nuts, and washers of wrought iron, ready punched........	15	$25 per ton
do gum refined,	15	10 per cent	Nuts used in dyeing, in a crude state	10	free
Myrobalan.........	20	free	do cocoa........	10	free
Nails, cut, and spikes	15	1 cent per lb.	do all those not enumerated, except those used in dyeing......	10	1 ct per lb.
do wrought, spikes, rivets, and bolts.....	15	2 cents per lb.			
do horse shoe.....	15	3¼ cts. per lb.	Newspapers....	10	15 per cent
do cut tacks, brads and sprigs, not exceeding 16 oz to 1000...	15	2 cts per 1000	Nux vomica........	10	free
			Oakum..........	10	free
do exceeding 16 oz to 1000..	15	2 cts per lb.	Oats..............	free	10 cts per bus
Nankeens, imported direct from China, as cotton.......	15	see cotton	Oatmeal....	free	10 per cent
			Ochres, or ochrey earths, when dry, not otherwise provided for.........	15	35c pr 100 lbs
Nankeens, not imported directly from China, subject to the regulations on manu. of cotton...	15	see cotton	Ochre ground in oil..	15	$1.35 per 100 lbs.
Nankeen shoes or slippers....	15	30 per cent	Ochre, brown, blue, red, and yellow earth, to be considered as ochre.....	15	35c pr 100 lbs
Napkins, cotton.....	15	30 per cent	Odors or perfumes...	20	30 per cent
Napt, or napped cottons, a manufacture of wool..........	15	30 per cent	Oil cake	free	20 per cent
Narcotin..........	15	30 per cent	Oil cloth for floors, stamped, painted or printed, valued at 50 cents per square yard, or less......	15	20 per cent
Natron.............	10	free			
Natural history, specimens of..........	free	free	Oil cloths, valued over 50 cents per square yard..............	15	30 per cent
Needles, sewing, darning or knitting	15	20 per cent	Oil cloth, not otherwise provided for	15	30 per cent
Needles, crochet.....	15	30 per cent	do Harlem........	15	30 per cent
Nets, fishing.........	15	30 per cent	do stones.......	15	20 per cent
Newspapers, illustrated....	10		do animal........	15	20 per cent
Nickel.............	10	free	do seal...........	15	10 per cent
Nippers............	15	30 per cent	do palm..........	15	10 per cent
Nitrate of barytes...	15	20 per cent	do cocoa-nut.......	15	10 per cent
do of iron......	15	20 per cent	do of cubebs.......	15	30 per cent
do of strontium.	15	20 per cent	do of cloves.......	15	30 per cent
do of tin.......	15	20 per cent	do of cajeput	15	30 per cent
do lead........	15	3 cts per lb.	do neat's foot and other animals...	15	20 per cent
Nitro mur. tin......	15	20 per cent			

	C. S. A. Tariff, 1861.	U. S. A. Tariff, 1861.		C. S. A. Tariff, 1861.	U. S. A. Tariff, 1861.
Oil, ricini, or palma christi	15	20 per cent	Ostrich plumes and feathers, manufactured	20	30 per cent
do castor	15	20 per cent	Oxymuriate of lime	15	20 per cent
do hemp seed	15	20 cts per gal	Oxymuriate, or chlorate of potash	15	10 per cent
do linseed and flaxseed	15	20 cts pr gal	Oxyde of zinc	15	1½c per lb.
do olive, in casks	15	10 per cent	Oysters	15	20 per cent
do olive salad	15	30 per cent	Pack thread	15	30 per cent
do rape seed	15	20 cts per gal	Paddy	free	50c pr 100 lbs
do all used in painting	15	20 cts per gal	Paintings and statuary, for the use of societies, schools, churches, &c	free	free
do kerosene and other coal oils	15	10 cts per gal			
do spermaceti, whale, and other fish oil, of American fisheries, and all other articles the produce of such fisheries	15	free	Paintings and statuary, as merchandize, not otherwise provided for	10	10 per cent
			Paintings on glass	20	30 per cent
do spermaceti, whale and other fish oil of foreign fisheries	15	20 per cent	Paints, carmine	15	30 per cent
			do dry or gro'nd in oil, not otherwise provided for	15	20 per cent
do all other	15	30 per cent	do water colors	15	30 per cent
do volatile, essential, or expressed, not otherwise provided for	15	20 per cent	do Span. brown, dry	15	20 per cent
			do Span. brown, in oil	15	30 per cent
Old silver, fit only to be re-manufactured		free	do terra umbra	15	20 per cent
Olives	15	30 per cent	do white lead	15	1½c per lb
Onions	10	10 per cent	Painters colors	15	10 per cent
Opium	15	$1 per lb.	Palm leaves, unmanufactured	10	free
do extract of	15	30 per cent	Palm leaf hats or baskets	15	30 per cent
Orange crystals	15	20 per cent	Pannel saws	15	30 per cent
do flowers	15	20 per cent	Pitt saws	15	30 per cent
Oranges	10	10 per cent	Pamphlets	10	
Orange bitters	15	30 per cent	Paper hangings, and paper for screens and fireboards	15	30 per cent
do peel	15	10 per cent			
do issue peas	15	30 per cent	Paper for printing newspapers, handbills and other printing	15	30 per cent
do flower water	20	30 per cent			
Ore, copper	5	5 per cent			
do iron	10				
Organs	15	20 per cent			
Ornaments, gilt, wood, gold paper, or for ladies' head-dresses	15	30	do antiquarian, elephant, imperial, demi, cap, letter, drawing, and all other papers not otherwise provided for	15	30 per cent
Ornaments not for head-dresses	15	30 per cent			
Ornaments, alabaster and spar	25	30 per cent			
Orpiment	10	free			
Orris root	15	free			
Osier, or willow prepared for baskets	15				

32

Article	C.S.A. Tariff, 1861.	U.S.A. Tariff, 1861.
Paper, all manufactures of, or of which paper is a component material, not otherwise provided for......	15	30 per cent
do wadding....	15	30 per cent
Papier mache, manuf. of......	20	30 per cent
Parasols and sun-shades........	15	30 per cent
do sticks or frames........	15	30 per cent
Parchment...........	15	30 per cent
Paris white, dry.....	15	35c pr 100 lbs
do ground, in oil......	15	$1.35 per 100 lbs
Parts of stills, of copper..............	15	30 per cent
Pasteboard.........	15	30 per cent
Paste giggers........	15	30 per cent
do almond.......	20	30 per cent
do perfumed.....	20	30 per cent
Pastework set in gold	10	25 per cent
Paste, imitation of precious stones....	5	5 per cent
Pastel or woad......	10	free
Patent mordant.....	15	10 per cent
Paving stones.......	free	10 per cent
do tiles, not otherwise provided for....	15	20 per cent
Pearl ash...........	10	
Pearl, mother of.....	10	free
do manufactu's of	15	30 per cent
Pearls, set..........	10	25 per cent
do not set......	5	5 per cent
do composition, set..........	10	25 per cent
do composition, not set......	5	5 per cent
Peas...............	free	10 per cent
Peanuts...........	10	1c per lb
Pebbles of glass for spectacles........	15	30 per cent
Pellitory root.......	15	20 per cent
Pelts, salted........	5	5 per cent
Pencils, black lead, camel's hair and red chalk......	15	30 per cent
do slate......	15	30 per cent
Pencil cases, gold, silver, gilt or plated..	20	30 per cent
Pen knives........	15	30 per cent
Pens, metallic.......	15	30 per cent
Pepper............	20	2c per lb
do cayenne......	20	3c per lb
do do ground	20	4c per lb
Perfumery, vials and bottles, ment.....	15	25 per cent
Periodicals.........	10	
Percussion caps......	free	20 per cent
Perfumes, all sorts...	20	30 per cent
Perfumed soap for shaving..........	20	30 per cent
Perry..............	25	50c per gal.
Periodicals and other works, in course of printing and republication in the Confederate States	15	
Personal and household effects, not merchandize, of citizens dying abroad......	free	free
Peruvian bark......	10	30 per cent
Petticoats, ready-made........	15	30 per cent
Pewter, old, fit only to be re-manufactured...........		1c per lb
Pewter, all manufactures of, or of which pewter is chief value, not otherwise provided for..	15	30 per cent
Phosphate of lime...	15	20 per cent
do of soda...	15	20 per cent
Phosphorus lights, in glass bottles, with paper cases.......	15	30 per cent
Phosphorus.........	15	20 per cent
Piano fortes........	15	20 per cent
do ferrules..	15	30 per cent
Pickles............	20	30 per cent
Picrotoxine, an extract............	15	30 per cent
Pimento...........	20	2c per lb
Pin, or needle cases, all..............	15	30 per cent
Pin cushions, silk, wool or cotton....	15	30 per cent
Pincers............	15	30 per cent
Pine apples.......	10	free
Pink saucers........	15	30 per cent

	C.S.A. Tariff, 1861.	U.S.A. Tariff, 1861.
Pins	15	30 per cent
do silver, iron or pound	15	30 per cent
Piperine	15	30 per cent
Pipe, cast iron, steam, gas and water	15	50c per 100 lbs
Pipes, clay, smoking	15	30 per cent
do watch, carre or cannon	15	30 per cent
do wood	15	30 per cent
Pipe clay	5	35c per 100 lbs
Pistols	15	30 per cent
Pitch	15	20 per cent
Pitch, Burgundy	15	20 per cent
Plains	15	30 per cent
Plaster of Paris, unground	5	free
Plaster of Paris ground	15	10 per cent
Plaster of Paris calcined	15	20 per cent
Plaster of Paris casts or ornaments	25	30 per cent
Plaster, court	15	30 per cent
Planks, wrought or rough	10	20 per cent
Plants	10	free
Plantains	10	free
Plants used in dyeing, in a crude state	5	free
Plane irons	15	30 per cent
Planes	15	30 per cent
Plated and gilt wares of all kinds	20	30 per cent
Platina, unmanufactured	10	free
Platina, manuf. of, or which platina is of chief value, not otherwise provided for	20	30 per cent
do crucibles	20	30 per cent
do vases or retorts	20	free
Plaits for hats or bonnets	15	30 per cent
Playing cards	20	30 per cent
Pliers	15	30 per cent
Plows	15	30 per cent
do plane	15	30 per cent
Plumbago or black lead	15	10 per cent
Plums	20	1c per lb
Plumes, ornamental	20	30 per cent

	C.S.A. Tariff, 1861.	U.S.A. Tariff, 1861.
Plush or shag, worsted	15	30 per cent
do cotton	15	20 per cent
do wool	15	30 per cent
do hatters, of silk and cotton, or of which cotton is of chief value	15	20 per cent
Pocket books	15	30 per cent
do bottles, green glass	15	25 per cent
Points, merino	15	30 per cent
Pole caps	15	30 per cent
do carriage hooks	15	30 per cent
do ferrules	15	30 per cent
Polishing stones	10	free
Pomatum	20	30 per cent
Pomegranate peel	15	10 per cent
Poplins, stuff	15	30 per cent
Poppy heads	15	20 per cent
do oil	15	30 per cent
do seed	15	free
Porcelain ware	15	30 per cent
do slates	15	30 per cent
Pork	free	1c per lb
Porphyry	15	30 per cent
Portable desks	15	30 per cent
Porter, in bottles	15	25c per gal
do not in bottles	15	15c per gal
Potassa, prussiate of	15	15 per cent
Potassium	15	10 per cent
Potash	10	10 per cent
do nitrate of, when crude	15	free
Potatoes	10	10c per bush
Pots, black lead	15	30 per cent
do blue	15	30 per cent
do cast iron	15	1c per lb
do melting earthen	15	20 per cent
Pounce	15	20 per cent
Poultry, prepared	20	30 per cent
Powder, gun	free	20 per cent
do black lead	15	20 per cent
do blue	15	20 per cent
do of brass	15	20 per cent
do puffs	15	30 per cent
do subtil. for the skin	20	30 per cent
Powders, pastes, balls, balsams, ointments, oils, waters, washes, tinctures, essences, or other compositions known as sweet scents, odors		

	C.S.A. Tariff, 1861.	U.S.A. Tariff, 1861.		C.S.A. Tariff, 1861.	U.S.A. Tariff, 1861.
perfumes or cosmetics, and all preparations for the teeth or gums.....	20	30 per cent	Quadrants and sextants.....	15	30 per cent
Powders for bleaching....	10	15c pr 100 lbs	Quadrant frames....	15	30 per cent
Powders, fulminating	15	20 per cent	Quassia wood.....	15	free
Precious stones, set..	10	25 per cent	Quicksilver.....	15	10 per cent
Precious stones, not set	5	5 per cent	Quill baskets.....	15	20 per cent
Precious stones, imitation of, set.....	10	25 per cent	Quilla bark.....	15	
Precious stones, imitations, not set....	5	5 per cent	Quills.....	15	20 per cent
Pressing boards.....	15	30 per cent	Quilting, or bed quilts cotton.....	15	30 per cent
Prepared vegetables, meats, poultry, fish and game.....	20	30 per cent	Quinine.....	15	20 per cent
Preserves, in molasses	15	30 per cent	Quinine, sulphate of..	15	30 per cent
Princes stuff, woolen	15	30 per cent	Rag stones.....		20 per cent
Prints or engravings	10	10 per cent	Rags of whatever material.....	free	free
Prisms, cut glass....	25	30 per cent	Railroad chairs, wr't iron.....	15	$25 per ton
Prisms of cut glass and metal.....	25	30 per cent	Raisins, Sultana, muscatel and bloom, in boxes, or jars.....	20	2c per lb
Professional books of persons arriving in the Confederate and United States.....	free	free	Raisins, all others...	20	1c per lb
Protractors, ivory mounted.....	15	30 per cent	Rakes, iron, steel or wood.....	15	30 per cent
Prunella.....	15	30 per cent	Rape of Grapes.....		20 per cent
Prunella and similar fabrics, not specified, in strips or patterns, of the size and shape suitable, exclusively for shoes, bootees and buttons.....	15	free	Rape seed.....	10	10c per bush of 52 lbs
Prunes.....	20	2c per lb	Rappers, brass or iron	15	30 per cent
Prussiate of potash..	15	15 per cent	Rasps.....	15	30 per cent
Prussian blue.....	10	10 per cent	Ratafia, a liquor.....	25	50c per gal
Pucheri		20 per cent	Ratans, unmanufact..	10	free
Pullies, iron, brass, copper and wood..	15	30 per cent	Ratans, manufactured or partly manufact.	15	20 per cent
Pulp, dried.....	15	20 per cent	Rattles, wood, ivory, coral or with bells.	15	30 per cent
Pumice and pumice stones....	10	free	Razors.....	15	30 per cent
Pumpkins.....	free	10 per cent	Razor cases.....	15	30 per cent
Pumps, stomach.....	15	30 per cent	Razor strops, wood..	15	30 per cent
Punches, shoe.....	15	30 per cent	Reaping hooks, iron or steel.....	15	30 per cent
Punjuns, Madras, cotton.....	15	30 per cent	Ready made clothing except wool.....	15	30 per cent
Purple brown.....	15	20 per cent	Ready made clothing of wool.....	15	12c per lb
do tin liquor....	15	10 per cent	Red chromate of potash.....	15	20 per cent
Putty.....	15	1c per lb	Red lead, dry or ground in oil.....	15	1¼c per lb
			Red chalk.....	10	
			Red precipitate.....	15	20 per cent
			Red Venetian.....	15	20 per cent
			Red Venetian, ground in oil.....	15	20 per cent
			Red wood and red sanders.....	10	free
			Red wool, or fur for hatting.....	15	10 per cent

35

Article	C.S.A. Tariff, 1861.	U.S.A. Tariff, 1861.	Article	C.S.A. Tariff, 1861.	U.S.A. Tariff, 1861.
Reeds, unmanufact'd.	10	free	Rugs, hearth or bedside	15	20 per cent
Reeds, manufactured or partly manufactured	15	20 per cent	Rum	25	.06 per gal
Reeds, weavers	15	30 per cent	Rum, bay, or bay water	20	25c per gal
Regulus of antimony	15	free	Rum, cherry	25	40c per gal
Reindeer skins, dressed	15	20 per cent	Russia, crash, hemp, duck, diaper, linen sheetings and other articles of flax	15	30 per cent
Reindeer skins, undressed	5	5 per cent	Rust of iron	15	10 per cent
Reindeer skins, tan'd	10	20 per cent	Rye	free	15c per bush
Reindeer tongues	free	2c per lb	Rye flour	free	10 per cent
Reps, natural silk and cotton	15	30 per cent	Sabres	free	30 per cent
Resin	15	free	Sadiron	15	1c per lb
Resin of jalap	15	free	Saddlery, coach and harness hardware, silver plated, brass, brass plated or covered, common tinned burnished or japanned not otherwise provided for..	15	30 per cent
Resin, nux vomica	15	free	Saddle hooks	15	30 per cent
Rest pins	15	30 per cent	Saddle trees	15	30 per cent
Rhubarb	15	10 per cent	Saddles	15	30 per cent
Ribbon wire, or cane-till, if covered with cotton or silk	15	30 per cent	Saddlery, all kinds not otherwise provided for	15	
Ribbons, silk	15	30 per cent	Safflower	10	free
Rice, cleaned	free	1c per lb	Saffron	15	10 per cent
Rice, uncleaned or paddy	free	50c pr 100 lbs	Saffron cake	15	10 per cent
Rifles	15	30 per cent	Sago and sago flour	15	50c pr 100 lbs
Rivets, iron	15	2c per lb	Salacine	15	30 per cent
Robes, made up	15	30 per cent	Sail duck	15	25 per cent
Rochelle salts	15	20 per cent	Sal ammonia	10	10 per cent
Rods and eyes of metal for stairs	15	30 per cent	Sal diuretic	15	10 per cent
Rods, wood, composition, casement, slit, or rolled	15	30 per cent	Sal soda	10	
Roman cement	15	20 per cent	Sal succinic	15	10 per cent
Roman vitriol	15	20 per cent	Salep	15	20 per cent
Roman candles	15		Salmon, pickled	15	$3 per bbl
Rope	15		Salmon, preserved in oil	25	30 per cent
Root, arrow	15	10 per cent	Salt, per bushel of 56 lbs in bulk	2c	4c
Root, madder	10	free	Salt, per bushel of 56 in bags	2c	6c
Roots, medicinal, not speci'ly mentioned, in a crude state	15	20 per cent	Salts of tin	15	10 per cent
Rosewood, manufactures of	25	30 per cent	Salts, Epsom, Glauber, Rochelle, and all other salts and preparations not oth'rwise provided for..	15	20 per cent
Rosewood, unmanuf..	10	free	Salted skivers, roans, pelts	5	5 per cent
Rose leaves	15	20 per cent			
Rose water	20	30 per cent			
Rosin	15	20 per cent			
Rosolio, a cordial	25	50c per gal			
Rotten stone	10	free			
Rouge	20	30 per cent			
Rubies, not set	5	5 per cent			
Rubies, set	10	25 per cent			

	C.S.A. Tariff, 1861.	U.S.A. Tariff, 1861.
Saltpetre, or nitrate of potash, crude	free	free
Saltpetre refined	free	10 per cent
Sandal wood	10	free
Sandarach	10	10 per cent
Sand stones	10	20 per cent
Sardines, in oil	25	30 per cent
Sarsaparilla	15	10 per cent
Sash fastners	15	30 per cent
Sashes, silk	15	30 per cent
Sassafras	15	20 per cent
Satin wood, manf. of	25	30 per cent
do unmanf.	10	free
Satin, all kinds	25	
Sauces, all kinds not otherwise enumerated	20	30 per cent
Saucepans, copper, iron or tin	15	30 per cent
Sausages, Bologna	15	30 per cent
Saws, mill, pit and drag, not over 9 in. wide	15	12½c pr lineal foot
Saws, mill pit and drag, over 9 inches wide	15	20c per lineal foot
Saws, cross cut	15	8c per lineal foot
Saw sets	15	30 per cent
Scagliola, tops for tables, &c	25	30 per cent
Scale beams	15	30 per cent
Scales	15	30 per cent
Scammonium	10	00 per cent
Scantling	10	20 per cent
Scantling and sawed lumber, not planed or wrought into shape for use	10	20 per cent
Scarfs, silk, cotton or wool	15	30 per cent
Scilla or Squills	15	10 per cent
Scissors	15	30 per cent
Scoop nets	15	30 per cent
Scotch braces	15	30 per cent
Scrapers	15	30 per cent
Screws, bed	15	1½c per lb
Screws commonly wood	15	
Screws, 2 inches or over in length	15	5c per lb
Scrsws, do, less than 2 inches	15	8c per lb
Screws, washed or plated & all others of any metal	15	30 per cent
Scythes	15	30 per cent
Sealingwax	15	30 per cent
Sea weed, and all other vegetable substances used for b'ds or mattresses	15	20 per cent
Seeds, garden and horticultural	free	free
Seed lac	10	free
Seines	15	6c per lb
Segars, all	25	
Segars, value of $5 pr 1000 or under		20c per lb
Segars, value of over $5 pr 1000 and not over $10		40 per cent
Segars, do, over $10 per 1000		60c pr lb and 10 per cent
Segars, paper	25	30 per cent
Seltzer water	15	30 per cent
Seneca root	15	20 per cent
Senna	15	20 per cent
Sepia	15	10 per cent
Sextants	15	30 per cent
Shades, lace, sewed	15	30 per cent
Shaddock	15	10 per cent
Shaving soap	20	30 per cent
Shawls, w'len, wholly or in part of wool	15	12c per lb and 25 per cent
Shears	15	30 per cent
Sheathing, copper, but no copper to be considered as such, except in sheets 48 inches long,14 inch. wide and weighing from 11 to 34 oz	5	
Sheathing metal, or yellow metal not wholly of copper nor wholly or in part of iron ungalvanized, in sheets 48 inches long and 14 inches wide and weight from 14 to 34 oz per square yd	5	free
Sheathing, paper	5	10 per cent
Sheathing and yellow metal nails,express-		

Item	C.S.A. Tariff, 1861.	U.S.A. Tariff, 1861.
ly for sheathing vessels...	5	
Sheetings, linen, hemp or Russia, brown or white...	15	25 per cent
Shells, gold, for painting...	15	30 per cent
Shells, silv'r, for painting...	15	30 per cent
Shell boxes...	20	30 per cent
Shell baskets...	20	30 per cent
Shell, turtle or tortoise	10	free
Shells, all other.....	10	free
Shellac...	10	free
Shell, manufactures of	15	30 per cent
Shingles...	10	20 per cent
Shingle bolts...	5	
Shirts...	15	30 per cent
Shirts and drawers, wholly of cotton, wove or made on frames...	15	25 per cent
Shirts, silk...	15	30 per cent
Shoes or slippers of leather...	15	30 per cent
Shoes or slippers of silk...	15	30 per cent
Shoes or boots of india rubber...	15	20 per cent
Shoes or slippers of prunella...	15	
Shoe stuff, or other materials...	15	30 per cent
Shot, gun...	15	1¼c per lb
Shot of lead for cannon, muskets, rifles or pistols...		free
Shot bags, leather...	15	30 per cent
Shot belts...	15	30 per cent
Shrubs...	10	free
Shuttlecocks and battledores...	15	30 per cent
Sickles, iron and steel	15	30 per cent
Side arms of every description...	15	30 per cent
Sieves, lawn, cypress wire and hair...	15	30 per cent
Silk, raw or as reeled from the cocoon, not being doubled, twisted, or advanced in manufacture in any way, and silk cocoons and silk waste...	10	free
Silk, in the gum, not more advanced in manufacture than singles, tram, and thrown or organzine	10	15 per cent
Silk twist...	15	30 per cent
Silk and mohair twist	15	30 per cent
Silk ribbons, galoons, fringes, laces, buttons and trimmings	15	30 per cent
Silk, value not over $1 per square yard	15	20 per cent
Silk, value over $1 pr square yard...	15	30 per cent
Silk velvets value not over $3 per sq yard	15	25 per cent
Silk velvets over $3 per square yard...	15	30 per cent
Silk, manufactures of, not otherwise provided for...	15	30 per cent
Silk, sewing, in the gum or purified ..	15	30 per cent
Silk aprons, collars, cuffs, chemizettes, turbans, mantillas and pellerines...	15	30 per cent
Silk and worsted valencias, toilenets, or crape de Lyons ...	15	30 per cent
Silk and worsted shawls, hemmed...	15	30 per cent
Silk and cotton vestings...	15	30 per cent
Silk bobbins or braids	15	30 per cent
Silk, caps, if entirely silk...	15	30 per cent
Silk cords...	15	30 per cent
Silk curls...	15	30 per cent
Silk floss...	15	20 per cent
Silk frizettes...	15	30 per cent
Silk garters, with wire and clasps...	15	30 per cent
Silk gloves...	15	30 per cent
Silk tossels...	15	30 per cent
Silk hats or bonnets for women...	15	30 per cent
Silk hat bands...	15	30 per cent
Silk handke'chiefs not sewed...	15	30 per cent
Silk hose...	15	30 per cent
Silk hose, sewed...	15	30 per cent
Silk lace...	15	30 per cent
Silk mitts...	15	30 per cent
Silk mitts, sewed...	15	30 per cent

	C.S.A. Tariff, 1861.	U.S.A. Tariff, 1861.		C.S.A. Tariff, 1861.	U.S.A. Tariff, 1861.
Silk, manuf with gold or silver, or other metals..........	15	30 per cent	Skins tanned & dressed of all kinds except calf skins....	10	20 per cent
Silk, pongees, white.	15	30 per cent	Skins, japanned, patents, or enamelled	15	30 per cent
Silk ornaments, oil cloth, suspenders, stocks, stockings and twist........	15	30 per cent	Skin ,fish,for sad'lers, &c..............	10	20 per cent
Silk watch chains or ribbons..........	15	30 per cent	Skins dressed with alum only........	10	20 per cent
Silk webbing........	15	30 per cent	Skins, sheep, tanned or dressed.......	10	20 per cent
Silk, all other articles not otherwise specified, made up by hands in whole or in part.........	15	30 per cent	Skins, goat or morrocco, tanned and not dressed..........	10	20 per cent
Silver bullion or coin	free	free	Skins, kid, tanned, dressed and not dressed..........	10	20 per cent
Silver, manuf of, or of which silver is of chief value, not otherwise provided for...............	20	30 per cent	Skins tanned & dressed otherwise than in colors, viz: fawn and lamb, known as chamois..........	10	20 per cent
Silver plated metal, in sheets or other form.............	20	30 per cent	Skins and raw hides of all kinds, dried, salted or pickled, not otherwise specified...............	5	5 per cent
Silver, German, in sheets...........	20	30 per cent	Skins, sheep, with wool upon them, raw or unmanufact washed or unwashed............	5	15 per cent
Silver, German,manuf or not...........	20	30 per cent	Sky-rockets........	15	
Silver leaf..........	10	20 per cent	Slate pencils........	15	30 per cent
Silver wire........	20	30 per cent	Slate, chimney pieces, slabs for tables, mantles, and all other manufactures of slate not otherwise provided for..	15	30 per cent
Sisal grass...........	10	$10 per ton			
Skates, costing 20c or less per pair......	15	6c per pair			
Skates, costing over 20c per pair......	15	30 per cent			
Skeletons............	15	20 per cent	Slates and roofing slates............	15	30 per cent
Skivers, tanned.....	10	20 per cent	Sledges............	15	2c per lb
Skivers, pickled......	5	5 per cent	Slick stones....	15	20 per cent
*Skins, pickled, in casks.............	5	5 per cent	Smalts..........	15	free
Skins of all kinds in the hair, dried, raw or unmanufactured	5	5 per cent			
Skins, calf, tanned..	10	25 per cent			

*In the Confederate States Tariff Act, as published, we find the following discrepancy : In schedule C, (15 per cent, *ad. val.*,) "Skins of all kinds, tanned, dressed, or japanned." In schedule D, (10 per cent., *ad. val.*,) "Leather, tanned, band, sole and upper of all kinds not otherwise provided for." As it appears to have been the intention of Congress to class most manufactured articles in the 15 per cent. schedule, we suppose it was designed to put manufactures of leather and japanned leather at 15 per cent.—tanned and dressed leather 10 per cent.—and raw and undressed skins 5 per cent.

	C.S.A. Tariff, 1861.	U.S.A. Tariff, 1861.		C.S.A. Tariff, 1861.	U.S.A. Tariff, 1861.
Snake-root	15	20 per cent	Sponges	10	10 per cent
Snaps, a clasp or ketch	15	30 per cent	Spoons, all	15	30 per cent
Snuff	25	10c per lb	Spunk	15	10 per cent
Snuffers	15	30 per cent	Spurs, all	15	30 per cent
Snuffer trays	15	30 per cent	Springs for wigs	15	30 per cent
Soap, all	15	30 per cent	Spyglasses	15	30 per cent
Soap, all toilet	20	30 per cent	Squares, all	15	30 per cent
Soap stocks and stuffs	10	10 per cent	Squills	15	10 per cent
Soda ash	10	free	Starch	15	20 per cent
Soda, preparations or manufactures of	10	20 per cent	Stars and knots of gold and silver	20	30 per cent
Soda, caustic	10	20 per cent	St. Ignatius beans	15	10 per cent
Soda, sal, hyposulphate of soda and all carbonates of soda, not otherwise provided for	10	20 per cent	Statues and statuary	10	free
			Statuary of foreign artists (as merchandise) not otherwise provided for	10	10 per cent
Soles, felt or cork	15	30 per cent	Statues, statuary, busts and casts of marble, bronze, alabaster, or plaster of Paris, and all specimens of sculpture, for the use of societies, colleges, schools, churches, &c	free	free
Souvenirs	20	30 per cent			
Spars	10	20 per cent			
Sparterre and willow squares for making hats and bonnets	15	30 per cent			
Spatulas	15	30 per cent			
Spa, or spaware	25	30 per cent			
Specimens of natural history, mineralogy or botany for the use of colleges, schools & churches	free		Staves, for pipes, hogsheads and other casks	10	free
			Stave bolts	5	free
Specimens of natural history, mineralogy and botany	10	free	Steel in bars, sheets and plates, not farther advanced in manufacture than by rolling, and cast steel in bars	10	
Specimens, anatomical preparation	15	30 per cent	Steel, in ingots, bars, sheets, or wire, not less than 1 inch in diameter, valued at 7c per lb or less	10	1½c per lb
Spectacle cases, all	15	30 per cent			
Spectacle glasses	15	30 per cent			
Spectacles, all	15	30 per cent			
Spelter, manufact. of	15	30 per cent			
Spelter in pigs or blocks	5	$1 pr 100 lbs	Steel above 7c per lb and not over 11c	10	2c per lb
Spelter, sheets	5	1½c per lb	Steel in any form, not otherwise provided for	15	20 per cent
Spermaceti oil, of foreign fisheries	15	20 per cent			
Spices of all kinds not otherwise provided for	20	20 per cent	Steel pens	15	30 per cent
Spirits of turpentine	15	20 pr cent and 10c per gal	Steel manuf or partly manuf not otherwise provided for	15	30 per cent
Spirits, all, except brandy, first proof	25	40c per gal	Stereotype plates	15	20 per cent
Spirituous liquors not enumerated	25	33⅓ per cent	Stiffners for cravats	15	30 per cent
			Still bottoms	15	20 per cent
Spokeshaves	15	30 per cent	Still worms	15	30 per cent
Spokes	15	30 per cent	Stockings	15	
			Stomach pumps	15	30 per cent

Article	U.S.A. Tariff, 1861.	U.S.A. Tariff, 1864.	Article	U.S.A. Tariff, 1861.	U.S.A. Tariff, 1864.
Stone ware, ornam'nt-ed	15	25 per cent	Sumac		10 free
Stone ware, common brown earthenware		15 20 per cent	Surgeons' instrume'ts		15 30 per cent
Stone ware not ornamented, above the capacity of 10 gals.	15	free	Suspenders, all		15 30 per cent
Stone, rotten	10	free	Suspender ends		15 30 per cent
Stones, building	10	10 per cent	Swan, down of		15
Stones, paving	free	10 per cent	Sweetmeats preserv'd in sugar, brandy or molasses		25 30 per cent
Stones, polishing	10	free	Sword knots, lace		15 30 per cent
Stone pumice	10	free	Sword knots, gold & silver		20
Stones, burr, manuf'd or bound up into mill stones	10	20 per cent	Sword knots, silk or worsted		15 30 per cent
Stones not merchantable, as ballast		10 per cent	Shingle & stave bolts		5 free
Stoves & stove plates	15	1c per lb	Tacks, brads, &c., not exceeding 16 oz to the thousand		15 2c per 1000
Storax (a balsam)	20	30 per cent	Tacks, brads, &c., exceeding 16 oz to the thousand		15 2c per lb
Straw baskets	15	30 per cent	Table tops, &c., scaglio, and composition		25 30 per cent
Straw hats and bonnets	15		Table, irons		15 1c per lb
Straw, for hats, in natural state		10 20 per cent	Tale		10 free
Stretchers for umbrellas and parasols		15 30 per cent	Tallow		10 1c per lb
Strings for musical instrum'nts, whip-gut or cat-gut		15 20 per cent	Tallow candles		15 2c per lb
Strontia		15 20 per cent	Tamarinds		20 10 per cent
Strychnine		15 20 per cent	Tamarinds, preserved		25 30 per cent
Studs, all		30 per cent	Tamboreens		15 20 per cent
Succory, ground		15 20 per cent	Tannin, medicinal		15 g0 per cent
Sugar, of all kinds	20		Tanning, extracts and decoctions for		10
Sugar in the raw state		¾c per lb	Tanning, all articles for, not otherwise provided for		5
Sugar, white & clayed when advanced and not refined	20	¾c per lb	Tapers, paper, with cotton wicks		15 30 per cent
Sugar, refined	20	2c per lb	Tapers, spermaceti, stearine or wax		15 8c per lb
Sugar, colored, tinctured, &c	20	4c per lb	Tapioca		15 10 per cent
Sugar of lead	15	3c per lb	Tares		20 per cent
Sugar, syrup of	20	¾c per lb	Tar, Barbadoes, crude		15 20 per cent
Sugar moulds, hooped or not		15 30 per cent	Tar, coal		15 20 per cent
Sulphate of alumina		15 50c pr 100 lbs	Tarpaulins		15 20 per cent
do barytes, cr'de or refined		15 20 per cent	Tartrate of antimony		15 20 per cent
do zinc		15 20 per cent	Tassels, silk		15 30 per cent
do Ammonia	10		Tassels, gold & silver		20 30 per cent
do lime, ungr'd	5	free	Teas, all kinds, direct from China or plac's of their growth		10 free
do of quinine & magnesia		15 20 per cent	Teazles		10 10 per cent
Sulphur, crude	free	free	Teeth, elephants'		10 free
Sulphur, flower of	10	20 per cent	Teeth, manufactured		15 10 per cent
Sulphuric ether		15 20 per cent	Telescopes		15 30 per cent
			Tentenegue unmanuf		5

	C.S.A. Tariff 1861.	U.S.A. Tariff 1861.		C.S.A. Tariff 1861.	U.S.A. Tariff 1861.
Terne tin, in plates or in sheets.......	10	10 per cent	Tin, manufacsures of, or of which tin is of chief value, not otherwise provided for............	15	30 per cent
Terra japonica......	10	free	Tinctures, odoriferous	20	30 per cent
Terra desienna, in oil	15	30 per cent	Tinctures, medincinal	20	30 per cent
Terra umbra.......	15	20 per cent	Tippets, fur.........	15	30 per cent
Tentenegue, in sheets	5	1½c per lb	Tobacco, leaves, unmanufactured.....	10	25 per cent
Tentenegue, in pigs or blocks, unmanuf	5	$1 pr 100 lbs	Tobacco, all manuf of	25	
Textile fabrics of ev'y description not otherwise provided for..............	15		Tobacco, all manufactured or unmanuf..		30 per cent
Theriaque..........	15	20 per cent	Toilet, glasses.......	15	30 per cent
Thibet, unmanuf, not provided for......	10	(see wool)	Tolu, balsam of......	15	30 per cent
Thibet shawls, real or goats hair.......	15	30 per cent	Tongues, reindeer	free	2c per lb
Thibet shawls body cotton with worst'd fringe.............	15	30 per cent	Tongues and sounds..	free	2c per lb
Thimbles, all........	15	30 per cent	Tongues, neats, smok'd	free	2c per lb
Thread of cotton, spool and other....	15	30 per cent	Tonqua beans.......	15	10 per cent
Thread, escutcheons.	15	30 per cent	Tools and implements of trade of persons arriving in the C. S. or U.S., not including machinery or articles imp'rted for manuf establishm'ts or on sale.........	free	free
Thread, flax or linen.	15	30 per cent			
Thread, pack........	15	30 per cent			
Thread, laces and inserting...........	15	20 per cent			
Tiles, marble.......	15	30 per cent	Tooth brushes.......	20	30 per cent
Tiles, encaustic......	15	30 per cent	Topaz, real or imitation	5	5 per cent
Tiles, paving and roofing of clay.........	10		Topaz, set..........	10	25 per cent
Tiles, paving and roofing, not otherwise provided for......	15	20 per cent	Tortoise and other shells unmanufact'd	10	
Timber, hewn or sawed, and timber to be used in building wharves..........	10	20 per cent	Tow of hemp........	10	$10 per ton
Tin in bars.........	5	free	Tow of flax.	10	$5 per ton
Tin, block..........	5	free	Toys, all kinds.......	15	30 per cent
Tin boxes..........	15	30 per cent	Trays and waiters, all	15	30 per cent
Tin, salts of........	10	10 per cent	Treacle, molasses....	20	2c per gal
Tin, crystals of......	10	10 per cent	Tresses, lace.........	15	30 per cent
Tin foil............	10	10 per cent	Tresses and wings of gold, silver, etc....	20	30 per cent
Tin, granulated	10	10 per cent	Trees, shrubs, bulbs, roots and plants not otherwise provided for.................	10	free
Tin grain	10	10 per cent			
Tin, liquor.........	15	10 per cent	Trimmings, silk.... .	15	30 per cent
Tin, muriate of	15	10 per cent	Trusses.............	15	30 per cent
Tin oxide of........	15	10 per cent	Tubes, iron, for steam gas and water.....	15	2c per lb
Tin in pigs.........	5	free	Tug buckles, as saddlery...........	15	30 per cent
Tin in plates or sh'ts	10	10 per cent	Turmeric......... ...	10	free
Tin in plates galvanized.............	10	2c per lb	Turpentine, spirits...	15	20 pr cent and 10c per gal
Tin ore............	5	10 per cent	Turtle, green........	15	10 per cent
			Tweezers, all........	15	30 per cent

Article	U.S.A. Tariff, 1861.	U.S.A. Tariff, 1861.	Article	U.S.A. Tariff, 1861.	U.S.A. Tariff, 1861.
Twines & pack thread not oth'rwise specified	15	30 per cent	Vermillion	15	20 per cent
Twines & pack thread linen or flax	15	30 per cent	Vessels, cast iron, not otherwise specified	15	1c per lb.
Twist, silk	15	30 per cent	Vessels, copper	15	30 per cent
Twist, mohair & silk.	15	30 per cent	Vestings, cotton....	15	30 per cent
Types, new	15	20 per cent	Vests	15	30 per cent
Types, old, only fit to be remanufactured	5	free	Vinegar	15	6 cts per gal.
Type metal	15	20 per cent	Violins	15	20 per cent
Umber	15	50c pr 100 lbs	Violin strings, gut...	15	20 per cent
Umbrellas	15	30 per cent	do do wire..	15	30 per cent
Umbrella furniture..	15	30 per cent	Vitrol, blue or Roman	15	20 per cent
Valencias, wool	15	(see wool)	Vitrol, green	15	25c per 100 lb
Vanilla, plants of....	10	free	do white	15	20 per cent
Vanilla beans	15	10 per cent	Wadding, paper	15	30 per cent
Vandyke, brown....	15	20 per cent	Wafers	15	30 per cent
Varnishes of all kinds	15	20 per cent	Wagons and vehicles of every description or parts thereof....	15	
Vases, porcelain, containing flowers, with stands and shades	15	30 per cent	Wagon boxes or parts of	15	30 per cent
Vegetable ivory....	10	free	Waiters, all	15	30 per cent
Vegetable ivory manuf of	15		Walking sticks or canes	20	30 per cent
Vegetables, prepared	20	30 per cent	Wash balls	25	30 per cent
Vegetables used in dying, in a crude state	10	free	Waste or shoddy....	10	10 per cent
Vegetables, not oth'rwise provided for..	15	10 per cent	Watches and parts of,	10	15 per cent
Vehicles of all kinds or parts of	15		Watch materials and unfinished parts of watches	15	15 per cent
Veils, lace, cotton, silk, &c	15	30 per cent	Watch crystals	15	30 per cent
Vellum	15	30 per cent	do pipe keys	15	30 per cent
Velvet, cotton	15	25 per cent	Water pipe, iron....	15	50c per 100 lb
Velveteens, cotton..	15	30 per cent	do wheels, of iron	15	30 per cent
Velvet, silk, value not over $3 per yard..	15	25 per cent	do colors	15	30 per cent
Velvet, not over $3 per yard	15	30 per cent	Wax beads	20	30 per cent
Velvet, bindi'g, cotton	15	30 per cent	do bees'	15	10 per cent
Velvet, terry, or fig'd, in strips or patterns of the size exclusively of buttons..	15	free	do sealing	15	30 per cent
Velvet, binding, silk..	15	30 per cent	do shoemakers	15	10 per cent
do when printed or painted	15	30 per cent	Wearing apparel of wool	15	12c per lb and 25 per cent
Venetian red	15	20 per cent	Wearing apparel, of whatever material composed, not otherwise provided for	15	
Veratrine	15	20 per cent	Wearing apparel, in actual use in travelling	free	free
Verdigris	15	10 per cent	Webbing, all	15	30 per cent
Verditer	15	20 per cent	Wedge wood	15	30 per cent
Vermicelli	15	30 per cent	Weld	15	free
			Wet blue	15	20 per cent
			Whalebone, of foreign fisheries	15	20 per cent

	C.S.A. Tariff, 1861.	U.S.A. Tariff, 1861.
Whalebone, of American fisheries	15	free
Whalebone hats and bonnets	15	
Wheat	free	20c per bush.
Wheat flour	free	10 per cent
Wheelbarrows	15	
Whetstones	15	20 per cent
Whips	15	30 per cent
Whiskey, all	25	40 cts per gal
Whiting	15	25c per 100 lbs
do ground in oil	15	25c per 100 lbs
White lead	15	1¼ ct per lb
Wigs	20	30 per cent
Willow or osier, prepared for basketmaking	15	20 per cent
Willow, manuf. of	15	30 per cent
Window glass, broad crown or cylinder	15	see glass
Wines	25	40 per cent
Wines or imitation of	25	
Wire, iron, not more than ¼ inch in diameter, nor less than No. 16 wire gauge	15	75cts per 100 lbs & 15 pr ct
Wire, between 16 and 25	15	$1.50 per 100 lbs & 15 pr ct
Wire, finer than 25	15	$2 per 100 lbs and 15 pr ct
Wire, steel, less than ¼ in. diameter, and not less than No. 16 wire gauge	15	$2 per 100 lbs and 15 pr ct
Wire, steel, less than No. 16 wire gauge	15	$2 per 100 lbs and 15 pr ct
Woad or pastel	10	free
Wold	5	
Wood, manuf. of, or of which wood is a component part not otherwise provided for	15	
Wood, bar	10	free
do Brazil	10	free
do Braziletto	10	free
do Chessmen	15	30 per cent
do Camwood	10	free
do Carmaguey	10	free
do Dye, all, in sticks	10	free
do Fire		20 per cent
do Fustic	10	free
do Goncallo, aloes	10	30 per cent
do Jacks	15	30 per cent
do Lignum vitae	10	free
do Log	10	free
do Nicaragua	10	free
do Pernambuco	10	free
do Queen's	10	free
do Red Sanders	10	free
do Rio de la Hache	10	free
do Santa Martha	10	free
do Sandal, in sticks, dust or powder	10	free
do Quassia	15	free
do Rose, satin, cedar, box, granadilla, ebony, lignum vitae, lance, mahogany, and all cabinet wood unm'nufactured	10	free
do unmanufactured not otherwise provided for	10	20 per cent
Wood, manufactures of cedar wood, granadilla, ebony, mahogany, rosewood, satin wood, &c.	15	30 per cent
Wool, unmanufactured, and all hair of the goat, alpaca and other like animals, unmanufactured, the value whereof, at the last port or place from whence exported, shall be under 18 cts per lb	10	5 per cent
Wool (as above) exceeding 18 cts and under 24 cts per lb	10	3 cts per lb
Wool (as above) exceeding 24 cents pr pound	10	9c per lb
Wool, all manufactures of, of every description, wholly or in part of wool, not		

	C. S. A. Tariff, 1861.	U. S. A. Tariff, 1861.
otherwise provided for	15	12c per lb and 25 per cent
Wool, manufactures of, if emboidered or tamboured, in the loom or otherwise, by machinery or with the needle, or other process not otherwise provided for	15	30 per cent
Wool, with other materials manuf. of...	15	30 per cent
Wool, stained, colored or printed, and all other manufactures of, or of which wool shall be a component material, not otherwise provided for...............	15	30 per cent
Wool, on the skin....	10	15 per cent
Woolen, delains, cashmere, muslin and barege, wholly or in part of wool, and all grey and uncolored goods of similar description....	15	25 per cent
Woolen cloths and shawls	15	12c per lb and 25 per cent
Woolen cassimere...	15	12c per lb and 25 per cent
do hats.........	15	20 per cent
do listings.......	15	20 per cent
do yarns	15	30 per cent
Woolen stockings, gloves, bindings...	15	30 per cent
Woolen bags........	15	30 per cent
do tippets......	15	30 per cent
Worms for stills.....	15	30 per cent
Wormwood, oil of...	15	30 per cent
Worsted stuff, all piece goods.......	15	30 per cent

	C. S. A. Tariff, 1861.	U. S. A. Tariff, 1861.
Worsted and silk shawls	15	30 per cent
Worsted and silk shawls, hemmed ..	15	30 per cent
Worsted and silk manufactures of and of mixed materials not otherwise provided for......	15	30 per cent
Worsted bags.......	15	30 per cent
do caps.........	15	30 per cent
do braces, hose, or drawers....	15	30 per cent
do plains........	15	25 per cent
do gloves	15	30 per cent
do mitts	15	30 per cent
do wove pantaloons.......	15	30 per cent
do shirts	15	30 per cent
do shag or plush, cut or not..	15	20 per cent
Yarns....	10	10 per cent
Yarns.............	15	4 cts per lb
Yarn, woolen and worsted, valued at 50 cts and not over $1 per lb........	15	12c per lb and 15 per cent
Yarn, over $1 per lb	15	12c per lb and 25 per cent
Yarn, woolen and worsted for carpets, under 50c per lb and not exceeding in fineness No. 14..	15	25 per cent
Do. do. do. exceeding No. 14 in fineness...	15	30 per cent
Zinc, nails............	15	30 per cent
do in blocks on pigs	5	$1 pr 100 lbs
do in sheets........	5	1½ ct per lb
do sulphate of......	15	20 per cent
do oxide of........	15	1½ ct per lb
do manufactures of	15	30 per cent

Sterling Money reduced into Dollars and Cents,

AT THE VALUE OF $4.84 THE POUND STERLING.

s. d.	$ cts.	s. d.	$ cts.	£	$ cts.	£	$ cts.	£	$ cts.
2 6	61	16 0	3 87	20	96 80	47	227 48	74	358 16
3 0	73	16 6	3 99	21	101 64	48	232 32	75	363 00
3 6	85	17 0	4 11	22	106 48	49	237 16	76	367 84
4 0	97	17 6	4 24	23	111 32	50	242 00	77	372 68
4 6	1 09	18 0	4 36	24	116 16	51	246 84	78	377 52
5 0	1 21	18 6	4 48	25	121 00	52	251 68	79	382 36
5 6	1 33	19 0	4 60	26	125 84	53	256 52	80	387 20
6 0	1 45	19 6	4 72	27	130 68	54	261 36	81	392 04
6 6	1 57	£1	4 84	28	135 52	55	266 20	82	396 88
7 0	1 69	2	9 68	29	140 36	56	271 04	83	401 72
7 6	1 82	3	14 52	30	145 20	57	275 88	84	406 56
8 0	1 94	4	19 36	31	150 04	58	280 72	85	411 40
8 6	2 06	5	24 20	32	154 88	59	285 56	86	416 24
9 0	2 18	6	29 04	33	159 72	60	290 40	87	421 08
9 6	2 30	7	33 88	34	164 56	61	295 24	88	425 92
10 0	2 42	8	38 72	35	169 40	62	300 08	89	430 76
10 6	2 54	9	43 56	36	174 24	63	304 92	90	435 60
11 0	2 66	10	48 40	37	179 08	64	309 76	91	440 44
11 6	2 78	11	53 24	38	183 92	65	314 60	92	445 28
12 0	2 90	12	58 08	39	188 76	66	319 44	93	450 12
12 6	3 03	13	62 92	40	193 60	67	324 28	94	454 96
13 0	3 15	14	67 76	41	198 44	68	329 12	95	459 80
13 6	3 27	15	72 69	42	203 28	69	333 96	96	464 64
14 0	3 39	16	77 44	43	208 12	70	338 80	97	469 48
14 6	3 51	17	82 28	44	212 96	71	343 64	98	474 32
15 0	3 63	18	87 12	45	217 80	72	348 48	99	479 16
15 6	3 75	19	91 96	46	222 64	73	353 32	100	484 00

Francs reduced into Dollars and Cents,

AT THE VALUE OF 18 6-10 CENTS PER FRANC.

FRANCS	$ CTS	FRANCS	$ CTS	FRANCS	$ CTS	FRANCS	$ CT	FRANCS	$ CTS	FRANCS	$ CTS	FRANCS	$ CTS	FRANCS	$ CTS
1	19	15	2 79	29	5 39	43	8 00	57	10 60	71	13 21	85	15 81	99	18 41
2	37	16	2 98	30	5 58	44	8 18	58	10 79	72	13 39	86	16 00	100	18 60
3	60	17	3 16	31	5 77	45	8 37	59	10 97	73	13 58	87	16 18	200	37 20
4	74	18	3 34	32	5 95	46	8 56	60	11 16	74	13 76	88	16 37	300	55 80
5	93	19	3 53	33	6 14	47	8 74	61	11 35	75	13 95	89	16 55	400	74 40
6	1 12	20	3 72	34	6 32	48	8 93	62	11 53	76	14 14	90	16 74	500	93 00
7	1 30	21	3 91	35	6 51	49	9 11	63	11 72	77	14 32	91	16 93	600	111 60
8	1 49	22	4 09	36	6 70	50	9 30	64	11 90	78	14 51	92	17 11	700	130 20
9	1 67	23	4 28	37	6 88	51	9 49	65	12 09	79	14 69	93	17 30	800	148 80
10	1 86	24	4 46	38	7 07	52	9 67	66	12 27	80	14 88	94	17 48	900	167 40
11	2 05	25	4 65	39	7 25	53	9 86	67	12 46	81	15 07	95	17 67	1000	186 00
12	2 23	26	4 84	40	7 44	54	10 04	68	12 65	82	15 25	96	17 86	....	....
13	2 42	27	5 02	41	7 63	55	10 23	69	12 83	83	15 44	97	18 04	....	....
14	2 60	28	5 21	42	7 81	56	10 42	70	13 02	84	15 62	98	18 23	....	....

Bremen Rix Dollars reduced into Dollars and Cents,

AT THE VALUE OF 78¾ CENTS PER RIX DOLLAR.

R. DOL.	$ CTS	R. DOL.	$ CTS	R. DOL.	$ CTS	R. DOL.	$ CTS	R. DOL.	$ CTS	R. DOL.	$ CTS	R. DOL.	$ CTS	R. DOL.	$ CTS
1	78	15	11 81	29	22 84	43	33 86	57	44 89	71	55 91	85	66 94	99	77 96
2	1 58	16	12 60	30	23 62	44	34 65	58	45 67	72	56 70	86	67 72	100	78 75
3	2 36	17	13 38	31	24 41	45	35 43	59	46 46	73	57 48	87	68 51	200	157 50
4	3 15	18	14 17	32	25 20	46	36 22	60	47 25	74	58 27	88	69 30	300	236 25
5	3 94	19	14 96	33	25 99	47	37 01	61	48 04	75	59 06	89	70 09	400	315 00
6	4 73	20	15 75	34	26 77	48	37 80	62	48 82	76	59 85	90	70 87	500	393 75
7	5 51	21	16 53	35	27 56	49	38 58	63	49 61	77	60 64	91	71 66	600	472 50
8	6 30	22	17 32	36	28 35	50	39 37	64	50 40	78	61 42	92	72 45	700	551 25
9	7 08	23	18 11	37	29 13	51	40 16	65	51 18	79	62 21	93	73 24	800	630 00
10	7 84	24	18 90	38	29 92	52	40 95	66	51 97	80	63 00	94	74 02	900	708 75
11	8 66	25	19 68	39	30 71	53	41 73	67	52 76	81	63 78	95	74 81	1000	787 50
12	9 45	26	20 44	40	31 50	54	42 52	68	53 55	82	64 57	96	75 60	....	....
13	10 24	27	21 26	41	32 29	55	43 31	69	54 33	83	65 36	97	76 39	....	....
14	11 03	28	22 03	42	33 07	56	44 10	70	55 14	84	66 15	98	77 15	....	....

PRUSSIAN RIX DOLLARS, REDUCED INTO DOLLARS AND CENTS,

At the value of 69 cents the Rix Dollar.

THALERS.	✳ CTS.	THALERS.	✳ CTS.	THALERS.	✳ CTS.	THALERS.	✳ CTS.	THALERS.	✳ CTS.
1	0 68	7	4 83	13	8 97	19	13 11	70	48 30
2	1 38	8	5 22	14	9 66	20	13 80	80	55 20
3	2 07	9	6 21	15	10 35	30	20 70	90	62 10
4	2 76	10	6 90	16	11 04	40	27 60	100	69 00
5	3 45	11	7 59	17	11 73	50	34 50		
6	4 14	12	8 28	18	12 42	60	41 40		

POUNDS SPANISH, REDUCED TO POUNDS AVOIRDUPOIS.

LB. S.	LB. AV'D.	LB. S.	LB. AV'D.	LB. S.	LB. AV'D.	LB. S.	LB. AV'D.	LB. S.	LB. AV'D.
1	1 01	7	7 10	40	40 58	100	101 44	700	710 08
2	2 03	8	8 12	50	50 72	200	202 88	800	811 52
3	3 04	9	9 13	64	60 86	300	304 32	900	912 96
4	4 05	10	10 14	70	71 01	400	405 76	1000	1014 40
5	5 07	20	20 29	80	81 15	500	507 20		
6	6 09	30	30 43	90	91 30	600	608 64		

AUSTRIAN POUNDS, REDUCED TO AVOIRDUPOIS POUNDS.

A. P.	AV'D. P.	A. P.	AV'D. P.	A. P.	AV'D. P.	A. P.	AV'D. P.	A. P.	AV'D. P.
1	1 23.60	5	6 18.00	9	11 12.40	40	49.44	80	98 88
2	2 47.20	6	7 41.60	10	12 36.00	50	61.80	90	111.24
3	3 70.80	7	8 65.20	20	24.72	60	74.16	100	123 60
4	4 94.40	8	9 88.80	30	37.08	70	86.52	200	247.20

POUNDS OF ANTWERP, ALSO, BELGIUM, BRUSSELS, GHENT, LIEGE, BRUGES, MONS, NAMUR, TOURNAY, LOUVAIN, MALINES, COURTRAY, ST. NICHOLAS AND OSTEND,

Reduced to Avoirdupois Pounds.

A. P.	AV'D. P.	A. P.	AV'D. P.	A. P.	AV'D. P.	A. P.	AV'D. P.	A. P.	AV'D. P.
1	1 03.35	5	5 16.75	9	9 30.15	40	41 34.00	80	82 68.00
2	2 06.70	6	6 20.10	10	10 33.50	50	51 67.50	90	93 01.50
3	3 10.05	7	7 23.45	20	20 67.00	60	62 01.00	100	103 35.00
4	4 13.40	8	8 26.80	30	31 00.50	70	72 34.50	200	206 70.00

POUNDS OF AMSTERDAM AND THE NETHERLANDS, ALSO, CURACOA,

FLANDERS, HOLLAND, BELGIUM, SURINAM, ROTTERDAM, THE HAGUE, UTRECHT, LEYDEN, GRONINGEN, LENWARDEN, HAARLEM, DORT, MAESTRITCH, NIMEGUEN, DELFT, ZEVOLLE,

Reduced to Avoirdupois Pounds.

A. P.	AV'D. P.	A. P.	AV'D. P.	A. P.	AV'D. P.	A. P.	AV'D. P.	A. P.	AV'D. P.
1	1 08.93	5	5 44.65	9	9 80.37	40	43 57.20	80	87 14 40
2	2 17.86	6	6 53.58	10	10 89.30	50	54 46.50	90	98 03.70
3	3 26.79	7	7 62.51	20	21 78.60	60	65 35 80	100	108 93.00
4	4 35.72	8	8 71.44	30	32 67.90	70	76 25.10	200	217 6.00

SPANISH AROBAS, REDUCED TO AVOIRDUPOIS POUNDS.

S. A.	A. P.	S. A.	A. P.	S. A.	A. P.	S. A.	A. P.	S. A.	A. P.
1	25.36	5	126.80	9	228.24	40	1014 40	80	2028.80
2	50.72	6	152.16	10	253.60	50	1268.00	90	282.40
3	76.08	7	177.52	20	507.20	60	1521.60	100	2536.00
4	101.44	8	202.88	30	760.80	70	1775.20	200	5072.00

FRENCH KILLOGRAMMES, REDUCED TO AVOIRDUPOIS POUNDS.

F. K.	A. P.	F. K.	A. P.	F. K.	A. P.	F. K.	A. P.	F. K.	A. P.
1	2.21	5	11.05	9	19.89	40	88.40	80	176.80
2	4.42	6	13.26	10	22.10	50	110.50	90	198.90
3	6.63	7	15.47	20	44 20	60	132 60	100	221.00
4	8.84	8	17.68	30	66.30	70	154.70	200	442.00

FRENCH LITRES, REDUCED TO AMERICAN PINTS.

LITRES.	A. PINTS.	LITRES.	A. PINTS.	LITRES.	A. PINTS.	LITRES.	A. PINTS.	LITRES.	A. PINTS.
1	2.11	5	10.55	9	18.99	40	84.40	80	168.80
2	4.22	6	12.66	10	21.10	50	105.50	90	189.90
3	6 33	7	14.77	20	42.20	60	126.60	100	211.00
4	8 44	8	16.88	30	63.30	70	147.70	200	422.00

LIST OF TARES

ALLOWED BY LAW AND CUSTOM.

Almonds, in cases	8 per cent
do in casks	15 do
do in double bales	8 lb. each
do in bales	4 do
do in frails	10 per cent
do in ceroons	10 do
do in bags	5 do
Alum in bags	5 lb. each
do in casks	10 per cent
Anvils, in casks	90 lb. each
Bristles, in casks	10 per cent
Butter, weighing from 90 to 100 lbs. in kegs	18 lb. each
Black Plate, in boxes	8 lb. do
Candles, in boxes	8 per cent
Candy, Sugar, in boxes	10 do
Cheese, in hampers	10 do
do in baskets	10 do
do in boxes	20 do
do in casks or tubes	15 per cent
Cassia, in boxes	actual
do in mats	{ 9 per cent, or 1½ lb for 4 mats.
Chocolate, in boxes	10 per cent
Coffee in bags	2 per cent
do in bales	3 per cent
do in casks	12 per cent
do in ceroons	6 per cent
do in boxes	15 per cen.
Cinnamon, in boxes	actual
do in bales	6 per cent
Cocoa, in bags	1 per cent
do in casks	10 do
do in ceroons	8 do
do in baskets	2 lb each
Cloves, in casks	12 lb do
do in bags	4 lb do
Cotton, in bales	2 per cent
do in ceroons	6 do
Composition spikes or nails, in casks	8 do
Copper	8 do
Copperas, in casks	10 per cent
Corks, in small bales	5 lb each
do in large bales	8 lb do
do in double bales	16 lb do
Cordage, Twine, in boxes	15 per cent
do do in casks	12 do
do do in bales	3 do
Currants, in casks	12 do
do in boxes	10 do
Figs, in boxes	10 do
do in mats	4 do
do in frails	4 do
do in drums	8 do
do in casks	12 do
Fish, Dry, in casks	12 do
do do in boxes	8 do
Flax, in bobbins	3 to 3½ lbs each
Gunpowder, in casks	23 lbs each
do in ½ casks	9 do
do in ¼ casks	5 do
Glue, in boxes	15 per cent
do in casks	20 do
do from Canton, in boxes	11 do
Hemp, Manilla, in bales	6 lbs each
do Hamburg, Leghorn, Trieste, in bales	no allowance
Indigo, in cases	15 per cent
do in barrels	12 do
do in other casks	15 do
do in ceroons	10 do
do in bags	3 do
do in mats	3 do
Iron, Sheet, in boxes	8 do
do Hoop, in boxes	8 do
do Russian Sheet, in packs	11 to 20 lb each
Jalap, in yellow mats	12 lbs each
Lead, pigs, bars, sheets, in casks	3 per cent
do White, in oil, in kegs	5 do
Lead, White, in oil, in hhds	100 lbs each
do do dry, in casks	6 per cent
do Red, dry, in casks	5 do
do do in oil, in casks	10 do
do Shot, in casks	3 do
Nails, in casks	8 do
do in bags	3 do
Ochre, dry, in casks	10 do
do in oil, in casks	12 do
Paris White, in casks	10 do
Pepper, in casks	12 do
do in bales	5 do
do in bags	2 do
do in double bags	4 lbs each
Pimento, in casks	16 per cent
do in bags	3 do
Plums, in boxes	8 do
do in casks	12 do
Prunes, in boxes	8 do
Paper, in bales	5, 6, 7, and 8 lb each
Raisins, in jars	18 lbs each
do in boxes	15 per cent
do in casks	12 do
do in frails	4 do
do in drums	10 do
Rice, in casks	10 do
Salts, Glauber, in casks	8 do
do Epsom, in casks	11 do
Segars, in boxes	13 do
do in casks	13 do .
Shot, in casks	3 do
Snuff, in casks	12 do
do in boxes	15 do
Soap, in boxes	actual tare
Spanish Brown, dry, in casks	12 per cent
do do in oil	12 do
Spikes, in casks	8 do
do in bags	3 do
Steel, in casks	8 do
do in cases	8 do
do in bundles	3 do
do from Trieste, in large size, in boxes	11 lbs each
do do in 2d size, in boxes	10½ lbs do
Sheet Iron, in casks	15 per cent
Sugar, Candy, in boxes	10 do
do do in tubs	15 do
Sugar, in bags	5 do
do in boxes	15 do
do in casks	12 do
do in barrels	10 do
do in mats	5 do
do in ceroons	8 do
do in canisters	10 lbs each
Starch, from Bremen, weighing 62 lbs each, in boxes	13 lb do
Tallow, in bales	8 per cent
do in casks	12 do
do in ceroons	8 do
do in tubs	15 do
Tea, Bohea, in chests	22 lbs each
do Green, (70 lbs and over) in boxes	20 do
do other (between 50 and 70 lbs) in boxes	18 do
do do (of 50 lbs)	20 do
do do (over 80 lbs)	22 do
Tobacco, Leaf, in bales	8 do
do do with extra cover, in bales	10 do
do do in boxes	15 per cent
Twine, in casks	12 do
do in boxes	15 do
do in bales	3 do
Whiting, in casks	10 do
Wire, in casks	8 do
Wool, in bales	3 do

* Extra allowance for hogsheads.
† Chest, so called, as now imported, but in reality quarter chest.

RATES OF FOREIGN MONEY OR CURRENCY.

	$ cts	Fractional parts of the Currency.	
Banco Rix Dollar, Sweden	39¾		
" " " Norway	39¾		
" " " Denmark	53		
Crown of Tuscany	1 05	20 soldi	12 denari
Curacoa Guilder	40	20 stivers	12 pfennings
Current Mark	28		
Dollar Thaler of Bremen of 72 grotes	71	72 grotes	5 swares
Ducat of Naples	80	100 grani	
Franc of France and Belgium	18 6-16	100 centimes	
Florin of the Netherlands	40	100 do	
Florin of the Southern States of Germany	40	60 kreutzers	4 pfennings
Florin of Austria	48½	60 do	4 do
Florin of Trieste	48½	60 do	4 do
Florin of Nuremburg	40	60 do	4 do
Florin of Fra kfort	40	61 do	4 do
Florin of Bohemia	48½	60 do	4 do
Florin of the City of Augsburg	48½	60 do	4 do
Florin of Prussia	22¾		
Florin of Basle	41		
Francisconi	1 06		
Guilder of Netherlands and other places—same as Florins			
Guilder, Brabant	33¾		
Genoa Livre	21		
Kobang of Japan	1 38	4 itzebou	1600 cani
Lira of the Lombardo and Venetian Kingdom	16	100 centisimi	100 millessemi
Livre of Leghorn	16	20 soldi	12 denair
Lira of T scany	16	20 soldi	12 denair
Lira of Sardina	18 6-1 0	4 reali	20 soldi
Livre Tournois of France	18½		
Livre of Genoa	18 6-10	20 soldi	12 denair
Livre of Catalonia	53½	20 sueldos	12 dineros
Livre of Neufchatel	26½	20 sols	12 deniers
Leghorn Dollar or Pezzo	90 76-100	20 soldi	12 denari
Milrea of Portugal	1 12	1000 reas	
Milrea o Maderia	1 00	1000 do	
Milrea of Azores	83½	1000 do	
Marc Banco of Hamburg	35	16 shillings	12 pfennings
Ounce of Sicily	2 40	30 tari	20 grani
Pound Sterling of Great Britain	4 84	20 shillings	12 pence
Pound Sterling of Jamaica	4 84		
Pound Sterling of British Provinces of Nova Scotia, New Brunswick, Newfoundland and Canada	4 00	20 do	12 do
Pagoda of India	1 94	36 fanams	48 jittas
Pagoda Star o Madras	1 84	36 do	48 do
Real Vellum of Spain	5	34 Maravedis	
Real Plate of Spain	10	34 do	
Rupee Company	41½	16 annas	12 piee
Rupee British India	44½	16 do	12 do
Rix Dollar (or Thaler) of Prussia and the Northern States of Germany	69	30 groschen	12 pfennings
Rix Dollar of Bremen	78¾	72 grotes	5 swares
Rix Dollar (or Thaler) of Berlin	69	30 groschen	12 pfennings
Rix Dollar (or Thaler) of Saxony	69	30 do	12 do
Rix Dollar (or Thaler) of Leipsic	69	30 do	12 do
Rix Dollar of Batavia	75	48 stivers	
Rix Mynth Dollar of Sweden	26½		
Rix ral Thaler of Gottenburg	27¾		
Roman Dollar	1 05		
Rouble, silver of Russia	75	100 kopecks	
Rouble, paper, of Russia		100 do	Varies from 4 roubles 65 kopecks to 4 roubles 84 kopecks to the dollar.
Specie Dollar of Denmark	1 05	6 marks	16 skillings
Specie Dollar of Norway	1 06	6 do	16 do
Specie Dollar of Sweden	1 06	48 skillings	12 'ore
Swiss Livre	27	100 centimes	
Scudi of Malta	40	12 tari	20 grani
Scudi, Roman	99 a 99½		
St. Gall Guilder	40 36-100	60 kreutzers	4 pfennings
Tale of China	1 48	10 mace	100 candareens
Tical of Siam	61		
Turkish Piastre	5	100 aspers	

TABLE

Of Foreign Weights and Measures, reduced to the American Standard.

AMSTERDAM.
	AMERICAN STANDARD.
100 lbs, 1 centner	108.93 lbs.
Last of grain	85.25 bush.
Ahm of wine	41.00 galls.
Amsterdam foot	0.93 foot.
Antwerp foot	0.94 foot.
Rhineland foot	1.03 foot.
Amsterdam ell	2.26 foot.
Ell of the Hague	2.28 foot.
Ell of the Brabant	2.30 foot.

CHINA.
Tael	1¼ oz.
16 taels 1 catty	1¼ lbs.
100 catties 1 picul	133⅓ lbs.

DENMARK.
100 lbs, of centner	110.28 lbs.
Barrel of toende of corn	3.95 bush.
Viertel of wine	2.01 galls.
Copenhagen or Rhineland foot	1.03 foot.

ENGLAND.
Old ale gallon	1.22 galls.
Imperial gallon	1.20 galls.
Old wine gallon	1.00 galls.
Quarter of grain, or 8 imperial bushels	8.25 bush.
Imperial corn bushel, or 8 imperial gallons	1.03 bush.
Old Winchester bushel	1.00 bush.
Imperial yard	36.00 inch.
Troy lb	144-175 lbs, avoird's.

FRANCE.
Metre	3.28 foot.
Decimetre (1-10th metre)	3.94 inch.
Velt	2.00 galls.
Hectolitre	26.42 galls.
Decalitre	2.64 gall.
Litre	2.11 pints.
Kilolitre	35.82 ft.
Hectolitre	2.84 bush.
Decalitre	9.08 qt.
Miller	2.205 lbs.
Quinta	220.51 lbs.
Kilogramme	2.21 lbs.

FLORENCE AND LEGHORN.
100 lbs, or 1 cantaro	74.86 lbs.
Moggio of grain	16.59 bush.
Barile of wine	12.01 galls.

GENOA.
100 lbs, or peso grosso	76.86 lbs.
100 lbs, or peso sottile	69.80
Mina of grain	3.43 bush.
Mezzerola of wine	31.22 galls.

HAMBURG.
Last of grain	89.64 bush.
Ahm of wine	38.25 galls.
Hamburg foot	0.96 foot.
Ell	1.92 foot.

MALTA.
100 lbs, 1 cantar	174.50 lbs.
Sama of grain	8.22 bush.
Foot	0.85 foot.

NAPLES.
Cantara grosso	196.50 lbs.
Cantara picolo	106.0 lbs.
Carro of grain	52.21 bush.
Carro of wine	264.00 galls.

NETHERLANDS.
	AMERICAN STANDARD.
Ell	3.28 foot.
Mudde of Zak	2.84 bush.
Vat Hectolitre	26.42 galls.
Kan litre	2.11 pints.
Pond kilogramme	2.21 lbs.

PORTUGAL.
100 lbs	101.19 lbs.
22 lbs (1 arroba)	22.26 lbs.
Carrobas of 22 lbs, (1 quintal)	89.05 lbs.
Alquiere	1.75 bush.
Mojo of grain	23.03 bush.
Last of salt	70.00 bush.
Almude of wine	4.37 galls.

PRUSSIA.
100 1 s. of 2 Cologne marks each	103.11 lbs.
Quintal 110 lbs	113.42 lbs.
Sheffel of grain	1.56 bush.
Ohmar of wine	18.11 galls.
Ell of cloth	2.19 foot.
Foot	1.03 foot.

ROME.
| Rubbio of grain | 8.95 bush. |
| Barli of wine | 15.31 galls. |

RUSSIA.
100 lbs, of 32 laths each	90.20 lbs.
Chertwert f grain	5.95 bush.
Medro of wine	3.25 galls.
Petersburg foot	1.18 foot.
Moscow foot	1.10 foot.
Pood	36.00 1 s.

SICILY.
Cantaro grosso	192.50 lbs.
Cantaro sottile	15.00 lbs.
100 lbs	70.00 lbs.
Salma grosso of grain	.77 bush
Salma generale	7.85 bush
Salma of wine	24.05 galls

SPAIN.
Quintal or 4 arrobas	101.11 lbs.
Arroba	25.16 lbs
Arroba of wine	4.11 galls.
Fanega of grain	1.54 bush.

SWEDEN.
100 lbs, or 5 1 spunds	9.76 lbs.
Kan or can	7.42 bush
Last	55.1 bush.
Can of wine	9.00 gal s
Ell of cloth	1.95 feet.

SMYRNA.
100 lbs, (1 quintal)	129.48 lbs.
Oke	2.81 bush.
Quiltal of grain	1.46 bush.
Quiltal of wine	13.50 galls.

TRIESTE.
100 lbs	123.60 lbs.
Stajo of grain	2.34 bush.
Orna or eimer of wine	14.91 galls.
Ell of woolen	2.22 feet.
Ell of silk	2.10 feet.

VENICE.
100 lbs, fresco gross	105.18 lbs.
100 lbs, peso sattile	85.04 lbs.
Moggio of grain	9.08 bush.
Anitara of wine	137.00 galls.

STANDARD WEIGHTS FOR GRAIN, SEED, &c.

Wheat should weigh	60 pounds	Buckwheat	52 pounds	Clover seed	64 pounds
Corn, shelled	56 do	Irish potatoes	60 do	Timothy seed	45 do
Corn, on the cob	70 do	Sweet potatoes	50 do	Flax seed	45 do
Rye	56 do	Onions	56 do	Hemp seed	45 do
Oats	36 do	Beans	60 do	Blue grass seed	14 do
Barley	46 do	Bran	20 do	Dried peaches	46 do

Fine Gold Foil,

GEORGIA
Sarsaparilla Compound,
OR
DENNIS' ALTERATIVE,
PREPARED BY
J. DENNIS, M. D., AUGUSTA, GA.

For Purifying the Blood and Diseases of the Liver,

In small doses, it is alterative and tonic; in large doses it acts generally as a mild purgative. In some cases it produces no perceptible action on the bowels, but removes, insensibly, impurities from the blood by its diaphoretic action, and greatly improves the general health.

If the Liver is kept in a healthy condition, and the blood pure by the use of this Compound Sarsaparilla, it will prove a great preventive of sickness, and great saving of expense in medicines, for the more it is appropriately used in a family, the better will be the general health of the family.

FOR FEMALES

It is excellent in diseases arising from General Debility, or a torpid state of the Liver, or in the most common diseases to which they are subject.

In Leucorrhea, or Whites, it has been tried and found a useful and invaluable remedy. It checks morbific secretions, removes the cause of disease by cleansing the blood of its impurities, and acts as a tonic to the system.

FOR CHILDREN

This is the best medicine that can be given, especially to those in a debilitated state of health, or troubled with worms. Generally a few doses given to a child when it first appears unwell, will soon improve its health, and render other medicines unnecessary. It is the general saying of those who have given it to their children that they have been more healthy since they have been taking it, but do not know whether it was the Sarsaparilla that improved their health or not. If this Sarsaparilla was not a superior medicine, this saying would not be so common.

It is approved of and recommended by eminent physicians, and brought more into popular use by their recommendations than by advertising. It may be relied upon as the Purest and Best in the market.

It contains in addition to SARSAPARILLA, the Hydro Alcoholic Extract of Queen's Delight, (STILLINGIA:) Grey Beard, White Ash, or Fringe Tree, (CHIONANTHUS:) Tincture of May Apple, or Mandrake, (PODOPHYLLUM;) and Blood Root, (SANGUINARIA.)

The publication of its ingredients and its natural taste and effects are its best recommendations.

For sale by Druggists generally.

FURNITURE WARE-ROOMS,

C. A. PLATT & CO.,

214 BROAD ST., AUGUSTA, GEORGIA,

MANUFACTURERS AND DEALERS IN

PARLOR, DINING ROOM

AND

CHAMBER FURNITURE,

IN EVERY VARIETY, AND UPHOLSTERED IN

Brocatel, Hair Cloths and Rep

ENAMELLED CHAMBER AND COTTAGE SETTS,

Cotttage and French Bedsteads, Hair, Cloth and Cotton Mattresses, Spring Beds of every style. In our Curtain Department, we have a large and beautiful assortment, imported direct from Europe, and we can confidently commend our Goods for inspection, as affording the very best assortment ever offered in this market.

BROCATELS AND SATIN DELAINES, IN NEW DESIGNS; DAMASK, IN ALL QUALITIES AND COLORS; LACE MUSLIN, AND NOTTINGHAM CURTAINS, SOME VERY CHEAP.

CENTER TASSELS, LOOP GIMPS,

PICTURE TASSELS, CORDS, &c.

WINDOW SHADES OF EVERY DESIGN,

CORNICE PINS AND BANDS, A FULL ASSORTMENT.

We are enabled, by our extensive Steam Works, to furnish, a t short notice, any article in the Cabinet line, as well as all kind of CAMP FURNITURE, such as Camp Stools, Chests, &c., &c.

We are the exclusive manufacturers and owners of

"PLATT'S ARMY CAMP CHEST,"

which contains every article necessary for the table and cooking for a messs of six, besides being readily converted into a table large enongh for eight, by simply raising two leaves. Also, "Painter's Camp Cot," which is one of the most convenient articles for the soldier in camp ever invented, being a fine Cot when opened, and when not in use making a roll only 6 feet long and 4 inches in diameter.

SHIRTINGS, SHEETINGS

AND

DRILLS,

AUGUSTA FACTORY,
AUGUSTA, GA.

Are prepared to supply, promptly, all orders for the following

STANDARD GOODS,

OF THEIR OWN MANUFACTURE:

4-4 SHEETINGS.
7-8 SHIRTINGS.
BROWN DRILLS, No. 1 (8 oz.,)
BROWN DRILLS, No. 2 (7 oz.)

The above Mills are capable of turning out 100,000 yards per week.

GEO. N. WYMAN & CO.

208 BROAD ST., AUGUSTA GA.

MANUFACTURERS AND DEALERS IN

CARRIAGES, WAGONS,

HARNESS AND ALL KINDS

OF

CARRIAGE FURNITURE.

A WELL SELECTED ASSORTMENT ALWAYS ON HAND.

—ALSO—

CHILDREN'S CARRIAGES, TRUNKS, VALICES, &c.
OF ALL DESCRIPTIONS.

www.ingramcontent.com/pod-product-compliance
Lightning Source LLC
Chambersburg PA
CBHW030720110426
42739CB00030B/1002